Ezra Townsend Cresson, Caleb Cresson, Charles Caleb Cresson

Diary of Caleb Cresson

1791-1792

Ezra Townsend Cresson, Caleb Cresson, Charles Caleb Cresson

Diary of Caleb Cresson
1791-1792

ISBN/EAN: 9783337109646

Printed in Europe, USA, Canada, Australia, Japan

Cover: Foto ©ninafisch / pixelio.de

More available books at **www.hansebooks.com**

DIARY

OF

CALEB CRESSON,

1791—1792.

Printed from his Original Manuscripts,

FOR

Family Distribution,

BY

EZRA TOWNSEND CRESSON,
AND
CHARLES CALEB CRESSON.

PHILADELPHIA:

1877.

PREFACE.

Caleb Cresson, the writer of the following Diary, gives the account of his own birth, at page 197, with various circumstances of Family History.

His first marriage with Sarah Hopkins, and her decease, are mentioned on page 199.

His second marriage with Annabella Elliott, the mother of his two sons John and Caleb, is related on page 199. Annabella Elliott was daughter of John and Annabella (Bonnyman) Elliott, formerly of Bolton, Leicestershire, England. She was born at Leicester, in England, 8th mo. 3d, 1743, and arrived with her parents in Philadelphia 5th mo. 27th, 1753. She deceased 10th mo. 12th, 1793, as related in the note on page 193.

On the 2d of 7th mo. 1795, he married Jane Evans, of Edgmont, Delaware County, Pa. widow of Thomas Evans, and daughter of John and Mary Cox. He outlived his third wife, and deceased at Philadelphia the 21st of 10th mo. 1816.

His father, James Cresson, deceased 3d month 23d, 1745. His mother, Sarah (Emlen) Cresson, deceased 8th mo. 2d, 1752.

It will be thus seen that he and his brother Joshua Cresson, (who was born 2d mo. 30th, 1744,) were left orphans at a very early age. They were adopted by their mother's sister, Mary (Emlen) Armitt, wife of John Armitt, who had no children of her own. She was as a mother to them during the remainder of her life. The feelings of love and gratitude, expressed in this diary, on the occasion of her decease, manifest the affection felt towards her by her nephews. A favourite saying with her was, "*It's poor living without Love,*" —which indicates her character.

Caleb Cresson took an active part in the affairs of the Society of Friends in his day. The old Book of Records, now held by the branch of Friends at Fifteenth and Race Streets, Philadelphia, is in his handwriting, as Recorder, from 1st mo. 16th, 1770, to 12th mo. 22d, 1799.

In person he was rather tall, (about 5 feet 10 inches,) slender, yet erect; of a dark complexion. Of courteous manners, though what would be called positive, or decided, in his character. His wife, Annabella, was small and slender in person, very meek and gentle in her character, amiable, and much beloved by those who knew her.

These traditions I have had from my Mother, Sarah Emlen Cresson.

He had two sons, John and Caleb, to grow to manhood, but left no daughter. John Elliott Cresson was born 11th mo. 11th, 1773; deceased 8th mo. 25th, 1814. He married Mary Warder, 4th mo. 28th, 1795. Caleb Cresson was born 5th mo. 11th, 1775; deceased 11th mo. 21st, 1821. He married Sarah Emlen, 6th mo. 4th, 1807.

His diary is written in a desultory manner, passing sometimes from subject to subject, without any attempt at connection or continuity. It contains records of occurrences evidently intended to be interesting only to his own family; and as he mentions (see page 34, under date of 5th mo. 13th, 1791,) intended only for family perusal. C. C. C.

2d mo. 27th, 1877.

THE DIARY OF CALEB CRESSON,

Began 1791.

NEW YEAR'S DAY, 1791.

I have thought that if persons who are so favoured as not to be under a necessity of labouring for a subsistence, would keep a Diary, or make notes as time daily passes—considering the well or ill spending of it of the utmost importance to our present as well as future happiness—such a practice might, on many accounts, be productive of benefit.

I am, therefore, now induced, although so far advanced on my journey through the wilderness of this world, to make a beginning in such an undertaking, and regret I had not began earlier in my day.

However, I am sensible it will require care, attention, and patient perseverance; nevertheless I am induced to set about it, though late, believing it may prove of some advantage and satisfaction to my own particular, in sometimes reviving things which would otherwise be buried in oblivion, and excite to the filling up the measure of our allotted duty in our short span of human life, which is afforded for the great and momentous end of working out our own salvation; and our blessed Saviour counsels to *work while it is day, for behold the night cometh, wherein no man can work.*

May we then press on with faith and holy confidence in Him who is alone able to begin and finish the great and all-important work to His glory and our peace and everlasting happiness.

I begin this Diary in the 49th year of my age—born the 29th day of the Eighth month, 1742—and although, as I have before observed, I think it a late beginning, I hope my dear children may not follow my example in that respect, but attempt it earlier, and I am fully satisfied they will not have cause to repent the labour which it may cost.

7th Day, 1st of First month.—This may be called seasonable weather, being very cold, a great body of snow being on the ground, which makes fine sleighing, and is reckoned a protection to the winter grain. The Lord's mercies are great. His sun shines and His rain falls upon the just and the unjust; yea, the most minute parts of His creation partake of His bounty. Let the earth, therefore, praise Him who provides for all, in time, and who will be the never-failing Source of Good to all His rational creatures in a blessed eternity, if they do but love, fear and serve Him.

The navigation of the Delaware has been stopped a week or two. Wood comes over on sleds, and from the west-ward by land. Oak, 32*s*.; hickory, 45*s*. is about the present value. Flour, 26*s*.; beef and pork, 4*d*. @ 5*d*.

Widow White, (mother of him called the Bishop,) deceased. P. Nicklin's wife, a youngish woman, died very suddenly, having been one of a jovial company the preceding evening, and a corpse in the morning: an awful instance, indeed, of the necessity of daily preparation to meet the undeniable messenger, as he comes sometimes with little or no warning.

1st Day, 2*d*.—Attended meeting thrice—afternoon at the burial of John Clifford's child, about four; uncommon for her forward parts and sweetness of disposition. Betsey Bringhurst, buried about 27th ultimo. She had been for divers years conversant in the school of affliction. A cancer in her side brought her to her end, which I trust, through mercy, was happy; bearing her great affliction and pain with much patient resignation, and it may be the impurities of early life were purged away by this suffering dispensation, which, though it was grievous, yet, I hope, was in great mercy and to enduring profit. She died beyond the meridian of life, in a single state, and, I trust, rests in the Lord, having escaped the pollutions of the world—*a great thing indeed*.

2*d Day*, 3*d*.—A pleasant day for the season.—Dined at Aunt Armitt's, with my wife and sons. She appeared pleased to have us with her, now in old age, (near 83,) having been a mother to me from infancy. Afternoon employed in writing, and a little carpenter work, which I reckon conducive to health.

3*d Day*, 4*th*.—At meeting for worship, and adjournment of monthly meeting, which held late.—Had several friends to dine with us, who remained during the afternoon.

4th Day, 5*th*.—A bad fit of the headache, which rendered me good for little. I have been subject to this disorder from childhood. May be it's my *thorn in the flesh*, and allotted to prevent an unprofitable and hurtful rest, which as pilgrims we ought not to aim at while in this state of varied probation and exercise. In the evening was enabled to attend with other friends who met on meeting business at our house, which, I hope, was not unprofitable to any concerned.

5th Day, 6*th*.—At High Street Meeting. Moderate—the snow goes fast, though the river remains shut fast with ice.

6th Day, 7*th*.—A moderate thawing day. Snow chiefly gone; dirty roads. Our beloved friends Mary Ridgway and Jane Watson, came to town from Wilmington, after visiting the families of Friends there. Attended a committee at Fourth Street House on Society affairs.

7th Day, 8*th*. Weather, mild forenoon; after blew up cold. Mother Elliott indisposed; went, with my dear wife, to see her in the evening. Was not idle this day.

1*st Day*, 9*th*.—Hail and rain this morning, which made the roads and streets so slippery as to be difficult to pass. However, I got to meeting three times, and was peaceful.

2*d Day*, 10*th*.—The cold abated so that I could more safely walk abroad. Wrote part of the day, and read the Holy Scriptures. Another part was spent in making some improvements in my writing room. The noble river Delaware continues fast.

3*d Day*, 11*th*.—At meeting in course, where our European women Friends were exercised in honest labour for our spiritual health. They think us too light and chaffy, nay, seem to think some very bad, and I fear they are not mistaken. O, for more devotedness in the greatest of all concerns. Afternoon, engaged in meeting business. Evening, with my wife to see mother Elliott, who continues poorly.

4th Day, 12th.—At meeting at Pine Street.—Jane Watson appeared in testimony—*I have desired to eat the Passover with you before I suffer*—a solid meeting. Afternoon attended a funeral. Evening at brother John Elliott's.

5th Day, 13th.—At meeting. Mary and Jane both concerned in testimony in the demonstration. James Cox and Elizabeth Shephard married. Afternoon, to see my old master, T. Clifford, who is indisposed.

6th Day, 14th.—Mostly employed in writing this forenoon. Afterwards attended a committee on Society concerns.

7th Day, 15th.—Attended to some outward matters. The ice in Delaware appears near driving—notwithstanding which the merchants have collected a great number of hands to cut or open a passage for the shipping from the point up to the city, which, 'tis said, they have effected.

1st Day, 16th.—Attended meeting, three sittings—that in the morning much favoured. Towards evening Margaret, wife of Jonathan Guest, buried; also, John Hill's son, a lad of about 14.

2d Day, 17th.—Rainy, snowy morning, with high winds—winter-like. Afternoon, attended Overseers' meeting. Caspar Haines' child buried.

3d Day, 18*th*.—A large week-day meeting; perhaps more so on account of the European Friends, who being poorly, were not there. However, we were favoured, T. Scattergood having the principal service. Evening at committee till 8. Ice in the river not yet broke up.

4th Day, 19*th*.—Employed in some domestic concerns and writing in my collection. I also read a little most days, in the Bible most frequently. I never was much given to spend my precious time in the perusal of light or unprofitable performances, but of later years I find I am not easy to employ myself in that way, as they leave the spirit poor, and take up too much of the room of the heart which should be devoted to entertain the Heavenly Guest. To them that open, says our Lord, I will come in and sup with him, &c.

5th Day, 20*th*.—At meeting. Performed some meeting business. Attended to some outward concerns. Evening visited a friend. Several vessels came up to-day.

6th Day, 21*st*.—Walked a mile or two out of town; found it windy and cold. Did some writing, and read in the best Book.

7th Day, 22*d*.—Was mostly in-doors to-day.—Wrote a letter to a friend in the country. Rebecca, wife of Samuel Morris, died; also, Nancy Flowers; of this young woman it may be said that the Lord was gracious to her, having, I trust, prepared her for His Heavenly Kingdom by judgment mixed with mercy, giving her to see the beauty of holiness, and the necessity to press after it in order to an admittance within the gate. Her illness was lingering, of the consumptive kind. Taken out of an evil world in much sweetness and peace, a little turned of 30. She has left an afflicted mother, to whom she was as a prop in declining life.

1*st Day*, 23*d*.—At morning meeting Cousin Jacob Lindly very eminent; afternoon, S. Emlen; evening, Thomas Follet. Mild for the season. Joseph Mifflin and Michael Eblin died.

2*d Day*, 24*th*.—Indisposed, yet did a little writing. This day my dear Aunt, who has been to me in place of a mother, was taken with her last illness, tho' she did not take to her chamber 'till the day following.

3*d Day*, 25*th*.—Attended our monthly meeting, which held late. Afternoon, attended the funeral of N. Flowers. Evening, was poorly. A peaceful mind is the greatest treasure; nothing worldly can purchase it.

4*th Day*, 26*th*.—Visited Aunt Armitt. Went to M. Eblin's burial. He was poor in this world, but I hope is made rich. A fine, moderate day. My son Johnny a good deal poorly, with a current complaint.

5*th Day*, 27*th*.—Was at High Street Meeting; Jane Watson and several others appeared. Afternoon, Hannah Wharton was buried.

6*th Day*, 28*th*.—Attended Philadelphia, or the Middle District, Monthly Meeting. A certificate granted for John Pemberton to go to England a second time on a religious account. Afternoon was at Aunt's; she now appears ill. Many people indisposed and dropping off the stage. Thus the living are instructed by the dead. There is no safety but in a constant preparation, but this cannot be obtained but by unremitted diligence; watch and pray continually, was the command. George Bryan, one of the Judges, died suddenly, of an apoplexy.

7th Day, 29*th*.—A cold morning. Aunt continues ill. Ice in the river again, which stops the navigation for the present.

1st Day, 30*th*.—Attended three meetings to-day. W. Savery much favoured at the last. How much labour is bestowed on the vineyard! O, for good fruit to the praise of the great and good Husbandman! Many sick, probably from sudden changes. Aunt Armitt now seems unlikely to recover, tho' she is favoured to retain her faculties tho' far advanced in age. Coarse, wintry weather. Cousin S. Emlen's black lad, Jem, fell through the ice in Schuylkill and was drowned. It is not good to withdraw from our duty on days appointed for public worship.

2d Day, 31*st*.—Was at Jonathan Dilworth's funeral. 'Tis said he met the messenger of death with composure and peace. Evening at Aunt's, who grows weaker gradually—appears peaceful and sweetly resigned. Thus ends the First month.

3d Day, 1*st of Second month*.—Attended our own week-day meeting; afterwards sat the adjournment, which concluded about 2. In the evening was at a committee on meeting business 'till ten—and was indisposed with fatigue. If we are in the way of our duty, we always have our reward, tho' 'tis sometimes wearisome to the flesh.

4th Day, 2*d*.—Visited a sick friend in the morning. Brother's family, several of them poorly.— Wrote a little and read a little. Our great Master requires nothing but what He gives ability to perform.

5th Day, 3d.—Attended High Street. Had a bad fit of my headache. Johnny a good deal unwell.

6th Day, 4th.—A snowy morning and a dull day, so I employed myself indoors, for I've always something to do, and I'm thankful for it, for I find employment keeps the enemy out; it likewise strengthens mind as well as body, especially good employment.— I hope I am sensible of the great favour I enjoy, not having to labour for outward bread.

7th Day, 5th.—Wet weather. Dear Aunt weakens fast, being now mostly confined to her bed.

1st Day, 6th.—Lodged last night at Aunt's, at her request, apprehending herself going, and wishing to have us, I mean my dear wife and me, near her. At the North Meeting in the morning; at High Street afternoon, and evening. M. Ridgway much favoured. How Friends in this city are watered and dug about from season to season. O, that we may bring forth fruit to His praise.

2d Day, 7th.—Lodged again at Aunt's, and continued to do so from this time forward 'till her death, she not being easy to permit us to go home. In the night we rose at her desire, but after a few hours she revived again, so as to take some notice of her friends, and dropped many good expressions from day to day, some of which we mean to treasure up. Quarterly Meeting to-day, but I did not go.

3d Day, 8th.—Youth's Meeting to-day. M. R. appeared greatly to satisfaction. Aunt continues, but is very low indeed. My son John better, which I acknowledge as a favour; also, brother's family.

4th Day, 9th.—Snow and sleet—a wintry morning; cleared up towards noon. Afternoon, John Head the younger, struck with a fit of the apoplexy on the wharf, and has not spoken since. Aunt continues, but to all appearance seems near the solemn close, yet very sensible and fresh in her inward and spiritual faculties.

5th Day, 10th.—Did not attend meeting to-day, being unwell. John Head remains to appearance insensible. Dear Aunt continues very low.

6th Day, 11th.—A fine wholesome morning, air being clear, and at N. W. My wife and self spend much of our time at our beloved Aunt's, whose present low situation requires constant attention, and she has every endeavour of those about her to render her trying situation as tolerable as may be, and being favoured with a peaceful mind, it is profitable to most that visit and are present with her, manifesting that the fruit of a well-spent life is humble hope and holy confidence in death, and she is enabled to meet its solemn approach without dread or terror, looking to and leaning on the arm of her beloved Jesus for help and support in a season so awful and interesting. Went to visit Cousin Rebecca Scattergood, who is ill.

7th Day, 12th.—Clear, hearty weather, tho' the river is full of ice. Called to see a friend in affliction. John Head died about 2 to-day; he was about 29, a merchant, in a single state, and the main prop of his father's declining years. A lesson of instruction is afforded by this awful providence, as it proves that youth and full maturity of strength does by no means exempt from the inevitable stroke. O, that we may be ready, having our loins girt and lamps trimmed, and waiting —I say *waiting*—for his coming.

1st Day, 13*th*.—Attended meeting at High Street morning and evening. Aunt continues in mutability, but in as low a state as well can be to live. In the afternoon the widow of John Jervis was buried—an aged woman.

2d Day, 14*th*.—John Head the younger buried. Aunt remains exceeding low indeed; has now and then kind of fainting fits. We are mostly with her, apprehending she cannot continue many days.

3d Day, 15*th*.—Attended our common week-day meeting. M. Ridgway appeared in testimony. We expected dear Aunt would have gone off this evening, but she revived again a little. It's a favour that she don't seem to complain of great pain, but at some particular times, tho' no doubt she feels great bodily weakness and distress. Takes little but water and a little jelly or sago, or such like. Nature, or rather the Author of nature, appears to be taking His inimitable workmanship gradually in pieces, to bring it to its original. Dust thou art, and to dust thou *must* return.

4th Day, 16*th*.—Had a bad fit of my old disorder, but got better in the afternoon. Josiah Bunting, of Darby, buried his wife.

5th Day, 17*th*.—Very windy, clear and cold; in the evening the cold intense, but owing perhaps to the very high wind, but little ice in the Delaware. Aunt evidently appears near the solemn close. The river froze over in one night, that is last night, all fast.

6th Day, 18*th*.—Our dearly beloved Aunt has had a painful and laborious night, but preserved in great patience and holy quiet. The Good Hand is evidently with her and supports her through the awful conflict. The Royal Psalmist seemed to possess his soul in holy confidence when he could thus exclaim or express himself: *Yea, though I walk through the Valley of the Shadow of Death, I will fear no evil, for Thou art with me; Thy rod and Thy staff, they comfort me. The righteous hath hope in his death.* About 9 in the morning she conversed a little with a near friend, and said: *He hath brought me to His banqueting house, and His banner over me is love.* About an hour after she said: "It's all peace; it's all joy *forevermore.*" These were her last words, (and in a low accent, but intelligible to those who were near,) except asking for a drop of water or something of that kind.

Thus she finished her course and slept in Jesus, about half after eleven in the forenoon, 6th day, 18th of 2d month, 1791, as a shock of corn, matured or ripe with age and laden with plenty, cometh in its season, having attained fully to her 83d year and a few days over.

Her pilgrimage might, or may be called even, steady, peaceful; having never had children, she escaped much of the care and cumber of life, and as she had had a good husband in his time she enjoyed many of its blessings and good things, altho' not in affluent circumstances, yet favoured with most of the necessaries and conveniences.

She had an open heart, was kind and sympathizing to the poor and those in affliction, entertained her friends at public times and otherwise, with much love and freedom. She was of a meek, loving, peaceable disposition, and loved the Lord and His Truth, I believe, above all.

As to her person, it was rather under or about middle size for a woman, not bulky, but rather spare; features very regular and agreeable, and in younger life was esteemed a very comely person.

She was married in her twenty-first year, continued a wife about thirty-two years, and remained the widow of one man about twenty-nine years, and was put into *his* grave, according to his and her desire, it having been dug very deep at first with that view.

Her corpse was taken to High Street Meeting House, (having been an elder about forty years,) and a solemn meeting held on the occasion, and thence to the grave, and committed to the solemn, silent enclosure of our original dust; nevertheless the spirit or immortal part, we doubt not, has ascended to the realms of light, life, peace, and joy forevermore, to join the Heavenly host even the redeemed of our God, who stand before the throne of immaculate purity, clothed in white robes, and palms in their hands, *saying: Amen: Blessing, and glory, and wisdom, and thanksgiving, and honour, and power, and might, be unto our God forever and ever—Amen.*

I have said less in this place on the occasion of my beloved relation's departure, as I mean to commit to writing a more full memorial of her pious life and peaceful conclusion, as I think her memory justly worthy of being handed down to posterity as a bright example for succeeding pilgrims, who are inclined to tread the path of virtue and true glory through the rugged wilderness of this world, if so be they may be mercifully preserved like her to escape the pollutions of time, and thereby be fitted for an abundant entrance into the joys of a blessed and never-ending eternity. And this is my earnest desire for all people.

7th Day, 19*th*.—Was much engaged at dear Aunt's late dwelling, in various cares about the burial. She appears, as she lies a corpse, younger than when in health—scarcely a wrinkle to be seen on her face—and might readily be taken for a person of fifty.

1*st Day*, 20*th*.—Did not go to Meeting to-day, but was mostly at Aunt's, many friends calling to shew their respect to the deceased.

2*d Day*, 21*st*.—Last evening our beloved friend Jane Watson had a sitting in Aunt's back room, much to our comfort and satisfaction; about thirty present. Through many tribulations the righteous enter. May *we* strive, and also be able.

This was the day of interment. Honour to whom honour is due, we find, is allowed, if not enjoined; and indeed she was honoured in life and in death. Many followed her to the Meeting House, which was so crowded that many stood. M. Ridgway and Nicholas Waln were concerned in testimony, and W. Savery in prayer. Weep not for her, but for yourselves and your children, who yet remain to tread the arduous steps of life below. She has attained the goal, having run the race, and through His might who is invincible, she is a conqueror and more, even in death. A large number followed her remains to the cold grave, though it was snowy.

3d Day, 22*d*.—Our Monthly Meeting in course, which I attended. Afterwards went to Aunt's late dwelling, and had a consultation with brother and cousin Ann Dawes about Aunt's affairs.

4th Day, 23*d*.—Attended Pine St. Monthly Meeting by appointment. Afternoon went to Aunt's, and, with others concerned, opened her will, by which it appears she has considered me as a son, and left me a child's share of what she possessed, with which I am satisfied, and desire to be thankful for the many mercies bestowed by the Great Dispenser of benefits from youth to this day.

5th Day, 24*th*.—At High Street Weekly Meeting. Our European Friends crossed the river this day, being pretty clear of ice, in order to be at Burlington Quarterly Meeting next First and Second Day.

Was engaged about some necessary employment in the afternoon. In the evening wrote a letter to Thomas Dobson and his wife, being old friends of my late dear Aunt, at New York, (which was one of her dying requests to me).

6th Day, 25*th*.—Attended to some necessary business at Aunt's, making out the inventory, &c.

7th Day, 26*th*.—Attended a committee on Meeting business, which took up a good deal of time.

1st Day, 27*th*.—At Meeting three times to-day; I hope not unprofitably.

2d Day, 28*th*.—Was taken up mostly in assisting in the division of Aunt's household goods, having one-third part.

3d Day, 1*st of Third month*.—Attended Week-day Meeting and a committee afterwards. Went on with the division in the after part of the day. Dr. Kuhn's wife died.

4th Day, 2*d*.—Completed the division to-day, and dismissed the remaining part of Aunt's family. The roads excessively bad, but weather moderate.

5th Day, 3*d*.—At Week-day Meeting. Afternoon employed in necessary business. Evening poorly.

6th Day, 4*th*.—Finished getting my things home. Attended to some affairs at home. In the evening, went to see a sick friend.

7th Day, 5*th*.—Was out on some business in the morning. Afternoon, on a committee at Fourth St. House. Evening, at home, writing. The weather mild, and likely to be wet. My brother's son, Samuel, born about 10.

1st Day, 6*th*.—At Meeting thrice. A wet day, tho' mild; wind southerly, which brings the frost out of the ground, and, I expect, will occasion very miry roads. Sister Gray ill with a sore throat attended with a fever.

2d Day, 7*th*.—Warm for the season; a gust in the evening, attended with sharp lightning and some thunder. Sister Gray continues ill; was there, with my wife, in the evening. My sons left off going to Dutch School at nights, for this season.

3d Day, 8*th*.—At our Week-day Meeting. Afternoon, employed writing, putting in order some of my dear Aunt's dying expressions, many of which are well worth preserving, and will be found in my collection.

4th Day, 9*th*.—Went on with the same business, and nearly completed a memorial concerning her pious life and death, which I copied fair, and handed among some of her relations.

5th Day, 10*th*.—Not very well, and, therefore, was easy to stay from Meeting, but was employed in reading and a little writing.

6th Day, 11*th*.—Dull, wet weather. Began to uncover my vines. Went to see brother's family.— Sister seems bravely for the time, having had a very favourable lying-in, her little son Samuel being fine and hearty. Went a good deal about town, on some necessary business, and did some writing at home.— Read the Bible some part of the day, which employment I find profitable many ways, tending to sweeten my spirit, and discourage the approaches of the grand Enemy; and I hope my dear children will be often conversant therein, being the best of books.

7th Day, 12*th*.—Markets are now scarce, and dear about this season, owing to a variety of causes— tho' fire-wood is reduced to about 30*s*. and 20*s*. per cord, the river having been quite clear for some time. Afternoon, attended a committee at Fourth Street House.

1st Day, 13*th*.—Attended three Meetings to-day. Mary Wood, an innocent young woman of 18, buried. She was taken into the North Meeting House in the way to the ground, being the first since it was built.

2d Day, 14*th*.—Rose early, and wrote as usual. Afternoon, attended Overseers' Meeting. Not very well this evening.

3d Day, 15*th*.—Rose a little after four, and was diligent in employment which may probably prove useful in future. Went to Meeting, and staid the preparative. Afternoon, to see a sick friend; afterwards attended to some domestic concerns.

4th Day, 16*th*.—Took a bad cold, and was poorly. A deal of wet weather, so that the Spring seems to come forward. The grass appears green before our door, and the buds swell.

5th Day, 17*th*.—The people don't forget Saint Patrick's Day, as it is called, and still make a mock of the poor Irish Saint, but if he is in Heaven it can't do him any harm. Wrote considerable in my collection to-day.

6th Day, 18*th*.—Up a little after three, and wrote a letter to my good little friend, Alice Needham, at Salem, New England, who made us a visit last Summer. Walked a mile out of town, for some orange trees and garden flowers.

7th Day, 19*th*.—A rainy day. On a committee in the afternoon at Fourth Street.

1*st Day*, 20*th*.—Attended three Meetings for Divine worship to-day, to my comfort and satisfaction. How much thou owest unto thy Lord! O, that I may be a faithful steward of His many mercies, which are very many.

2*d Day*, 21*st*.—Changeable, unpleasant weather, with high winds.

3*d Day*, 22*d*.—A fine, clear day. Being our Monthly Meeting, William Savery laid his concern before Friends to go to Charleston on a religious visit, which was concurred with and a certificate directed. John Skyrin and Ann Drinker, and Jacob Tomkins and Hannah Yerkes made proposals of marriage.

4th Day, 23d.—Employed improving my yard and border, and fixing my vines. Weather mild.— Wood much fallen in price.

5th Day, 24th.—Had a bad spell of the headache to-day, which confined me mostly to the house. Have nearly concluded to have my hair off, to see if it may not be a means of relieving me. An awful evening, by reason of the thunder and lightning, which was very sharp and loud at this early season of the year.

6th Day, 25th.—Rain in the night, which will forward the vegetation. The grass has come forward, and looks fine and green; some of the vines push out and bleed. William Kenly's son, a young man of 20, died suddenly, and was buried to-day; also, William Heyshan's wife, who also died very suddenly.

I went into what is called the Church burying-ground, and viewed the little spot that contains the earthly remains of Benjamin Franklin, once so popular, and noted in his day amongst the great and the learned, but death has now brought him on a level with the meanest. He made but little profession as to religion in his life, but I am told he thought it of some importance near his close, and so we must leave him in the hands of Infinite Mercy. His cold bed is close up to the north wall, near the north-west corner.

7th Day, 26th.—Our Spring Meeting begins to-day; many Friends from the country attend it. Was poorly, with a bad cold and some fever.

1st Day, 27th.—Was at three Meetings, which were favoured.

2d Day, 28th.—A little better to-day, so that I got out to Meeting, where some too forward spirits marred the work, tho' I hope some were benefitted by the opportunity in the end, as they waited in their own gifts, and looked to the Master in preference to the servants. My cold yet troublesome.

3d Day, *29th*.—But poorly—yet attended our Meeting in course, which was comfortable, Peter Yarnall having the principal service, who may be justly allowed to be a great minister. Being the adjournment of the Monthly Meeting, a certificate was signed for William Savery, and a minute for Thos. Gaskill his companion, on his intended visit to Charleston and some parts of the Southern Governments.

4th Day, *30th*.—Was poorly, and did not do much but read, more especially as it was in part a wet day.

5th Day, *31st*.—March, as it is commonly called, goes out to-day, and, according to the common proverb, like a lamb—that is, mild and moderate.

6th Day, *1st of Fourth month*.—This is vulgarly called April Fool's Day. How simple soever customs long established may be, there is a strange aptitude in the people to keep them up; several devices for the purpose of gratifying a vain and unprofitable vein of humour, were, however, ingenious enough.

7th Day, *2d*.—Bought some garden seeds, with a view of having something pleasant in my yard during the Summer season. Sowed and planted several things in the pots, for the ensuing Summer, and was a good deal engaged most part of the day. Cool towards evening.

1st Day, *3d*.—A cool morning for the season.— Ice in our yard of considerable thickness. My lemon and orange trees a good deal pinched. At Meeting three times. Tom Jacobs buried to-day.

2d Day, 4*th*.—White frost this morning, and clear. Hannah Haydock deceased at New York, 5th day, 31st ult., after a long illness of a consumption. She has, I think, left seven children.

The European Friends left town to-day for the Jerseys, and it is likely may visit New England before they return. Went in the evening, with my dear wife, to take leave of our valued and beloved friend, William Savery, who is going in Truth's service to Charleston by sea, with an intention of returning by land. May the Lord preserve him every way, is our ardent desire, and, I may say, *prayer*.

3d Day, 5*th*.—Attended 3d day Meeting, after which the adjournment of the Monthly Meeting was held. Afternoon was spent about some temporal business. Evening, went to see a friend. Am a little better of the cold I have had for some weeks. I find I have but a slender tenure in this mortal tabernacle. O, may I be prepared and fitted for a better inheritance, but it *will* be verified that *thro' much tribulation* we enter, and if at all it will be through infinite mercy—not of works, nor *of him that willeth, nor of him that runneth, but of God that sheweth mercy.*

John Gracey, an aged Friend at Haverford, deceased lately, more than four-score. Also, Jas. Jones, of Merion, aged 92, who had lived to prove the proverb, "once a man, and twice a child."

The weather mild. The winter grain, 'tis said, looks remarkably well. My apricot tree in full bloom.

4th Day, 6th.—Went to market for some garden seeds; afterwards took a walk to R. Morris' place (about three miles) for some vines, and when I got back was much wearied. Afternoon, was employed about some temporal engagements, which I hope may be useful to my dear children at least. The weather at mid-day pleasant, tho' I am informed there was frost in the night.

5th Day, 7th.—Rode to Henry Gurney's about business; afterwards brought Mother Elliott to our house. The roads mend so as to be tolerable in some places. Frost for several mornings past. Attended to the improvements going on in my yard.

6th Day, 8th.—Qualified at the Register's Office to act as one of the Executors of my dear Aunt's will. Read and wrote as usual, at intervals. Our dear friend William Savery sailed to-day for Charleston, on a religious visit to that libertine city. May they profit by his labours.

7th Day, 9th.—Attended to some domestic matters. My cold nearly worn off, having been poorly with it near a month. Read and wrote as common. Mother went home in the evening.

1st Day, 10th.—At three Meetings. Weather now pleasant, tho' the peach trees are not out yet.

2d Day, 11th.—Was about town on business.—Attended to my improvements at home. Our friend William Savery has had but poor winds since he left us, so that 'tis probable he may have what is called a long passage.

3d Day, 12th.—Attended Week-day Meeting; Thomas Fallet in testimony. Weather warm and growing. Rain afternoon and night, refreshing to the face of nature. Apricot in bloom. Set out my orange trees. Read and wrote at intervals to fill up precious time, so that when the audit—the great audit—comes, which must come upon all, I may not be ranked amongst the unprofitable servants. O, this would be indeed the height of misery!

4th Day, 13*th.*—April showers, which must benefit the creation. How blest is this land. Seed-time and harvest, day and night, Summer and Winter, are yet vouchsafed. *Praise the Lord, O my soul,* for He hath indeed *dealt bountifully with thee.* Even the smaller links in the creation, the blue-birds and martins, how joyous, skimming the air and chanting their Great Maker's praise. O, may the lord of the great system of nature, Man, the first in the order of intelligence, not be deficient, for greatly indeed are we indebted.

5th Day, 14*th.*—At Meeting at High St. Isaac Bartram and Sarah Shipley married. April showers. Esther, wife of John Morton, deceased. Riches cannot avert the stroke of death; all must submit at the appointed time. To be prepared is, therefore, of the utmost importance. See to it in good earnest, O, my soul, in this thy day.

6th Day, 15*th.*—A rainy morning; cleared away about noon, and was fine. My apricot tree has no fruit on it, tho' I have waited seven years in expectation—so have concluded to cut it down. May I not resemble it in a spiritual sense. Was busy, like Martha, to-day. About noon heard of the decease of our honest friend Robert Willis, who concluded a life of 70 and upwards at Joseph Kaighn's near Gloucester;

he was at our house about two weeks ago, cheerful and well. I trust he has now experienced a happy translation from works to rewards, having long been a labourer in the Lord's Vineyard, in this country and also in England. He was a plain man, like Jacob, *good at heart*, so he gained favour with man, and I hope with his Maker too.

Being obliged to use some expedient for my headache with which I am so sorely afflicted, I have concluded to cut off my hair, tho' it is a cross to me in some respects, to part with a natural covering for one which is not so. However, I believe it may be allowable in some cases, in order to obtain relief if it may be had.

7th Day, 16*th*.—I rose this morning between 3 and 4, and I never remember to have seen a finer dawn: the mildness of the air, the beauty of the twinkling luminaries, the healthful smell of the vegetating earth after a refreshing rain—all conspired to raise the mind in gratitude and devotion to the Bounteous Benefactor, whose will is that His children should be happy here and hereafter, and the great cause why they are not so, too often arises from their own imprudence and revolt from the Divine law impressed on every mind, and that sense of obligation and duty made known in the secret of the heart—for if this were enough attended to and obeyed, it would prove the high road to felicity, both in this world and the next.

1st Day, 17*th*.—Rose early, and with Johnny and Caleb, my two sons, crossed the Delaware to J. Kaighn's, in order to be at the burial of Robt. Willis,

Jn: Elliott Cresson.

- 12 Mo. 7th 1796

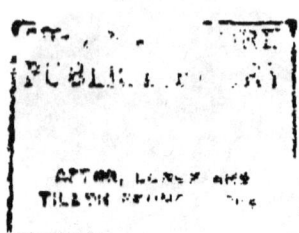

who was buried at Newtown, after a solid Meeting. We returned about 4, and attended evening Meeting at High Street.

2d Day, 18*th*.—The weather settled and fair. Wind fixed in the western board. Attended Overseers' Meeting afternoon. We think and talk of dear William Savery, and hope he is in Charleston by this time.

3d Day, 19*th*.—Rose early. Weather favourable for the improvements I have in hand. Attended Week-day Meeting in course; Preparative Meeting afterwards, which sat late. Afternoon was much engaged: evening, went to see some friends. Cool and windy.

4th Day, 20*th*.—Much employed this morning. The vegetation much advanced; peach and plum trees in full bloom; vines shot about an inch—some more. They look hearty; perhaps I may have a little fruit, to distinguish the kinds. My dear wife and I went to see some friends in the afternoon and evening. I am now favoured to feel pretty comfortable and well in health.

5th Day, 21*st*.—A thick fog obscured the sunbeams, tho' it broke out about 10, and continued clear till towards evening, when it rained a little; growing weather. Nailed up some of my vines. Attended to some workmen I have employed, who generally require attention, if we expect things done to good purpose. In-doors most of the day, and favoured to feel pretty well.

6th Day, 22*d*.—Up about 4. Read and wrote in my collection, then did some out-doors work.—

Weather, clouds and sun alternately; warm enough to be pleasant and growing. The Great Benefactor cares for His whole creation, and causes His rain to descend upon the just and the unjust. May we all prize and adore His mercy and goodness, who waits long upon the children of men, to see if there be any that will return and seek the Lord.

This is called by some Good Friday, and if I preferred one day to another, or considered one day more holy than another, it would be this day, on which it is supposed our blessed Saviour suffered without the gates of Jerusalem, a propitiatory sacrifice for the sins of mankind.

7th Day, 23d.—My poor head was very sick to-day, which continued 'till towards evening, and made the bed the most proper place for me most part of the day. Could eat nothing 'till afternoon. May be this affliction of the sick headache is ordered in wisdom, to keep me humble, and under a proper sense of my insignificance in the world, of myself, and entire dependence on the Great Creator and Benefactor for every blessing.

I think 'tis near time to sow and plant some flower seeds, which I have found do best if put in the ground about the beginning of the Fifth month. The Fourth is commonly too cold for tender flowers, which, if they get stunted, seldom recover. A growing rain in the evening and night. How the creation rejoices in the Almighty's bounty.

1st Day, 24th.—This is called Easter Sunday, by the Episcopalians, Lutherans and Calvinists, and I hope by some kept sincerely to the Lord as a holy day, on account of our blessed Saviour's resurrection from the dead. A dull, growing morning.

2d Day, 25*th*.—To see a friend from Jersey, who is afflicted with a cancer in his breast, of long standing, and is here in town under the doctor's hand.— What numerous evils the human frame is subject to, and how thankful ought those to be who are exempt from such heavy dispensations of suffering with which very many of our fellow-creatures are conversant.

3d Day, 26*th*.—Up nearly with the sun. Walked to Springettsbury, about some stone for our water-cistern; returned to breakfast. My son Caleb and I had a very pleasant walk—nature being in her gayest dress. Heard of the decease of Rebecca Chambers, of London Grove, who was buried to-day. Sydney Morrison deceased. Attended our Monthly Meeting in course, which sat 'till about 2.

4th Day, 27*th*.—Engaged about some improvements, viz. a water-cistern, a sink out of the kitchen, and raising my yard a little higher. Much fatigued in the evening.

5th Day, 28*th*.—A pleasant, but cool, morning. Attended Week-day Meeting at High Street. Afterwards finished sowing and planting flower seeds. Put down 500 herring to-day, from Schuylkill, which some apprehend are the best.

6th Day, 29*th*.—Attended to my outward affairs most part of this day.

7th Day, 30*th*.—Employed much as the former, tho' did not neglect to read a portion of Holy Writ.

1st Day, 1st of Fifth month.—May Day, and a fine one it really is. Warm enough to be pleasant, and at first thought we might suppose such weather, were it to continue, would be most agreeable, but experience teaches (and nothing more effectually,) that the vicissitudes of cold and heat, fair and foul weather, are ordered in wisdom incomprehensible, to render us the more happy, (if all is well within,) for by a contrast we are taught more to prize present good, when we have to experience the effect of what is contrary thereto; and if evil, or things which cross our inclination, are permitted, then to stand in the resignation is best, having confidence in the Divine promise that all things shall work together for good to them who love and fear the Great Name. Let us then, in this perilous wilderness, lean on the Almighty Arm of Power, doing all we can to keep a conscience void of offence towards all men, and more especially towards our Great Creator and Benefactor. Then will things eventually work together for good, and, if we do not see it at the present, time will unfold how much it is for our profit. The husbandman waiteth, and hath long patience, so must we, for we cannot sow and reap both at once—there must be a time for increase. Let us then not be discouraged, but trust. Trust in the Almighty, who will order all things for the best, and we shall find that nothing shall harm us, if we are in sincerity followers of that which is good.

2d Day, 2d.—Our Quarterly Meeting, where diversity of sentiment appeared, but being preserved in the quietude, peace was preserved, which is the most desirable of all things.

3d Day, 3d.—Our Youth's Meeting to-day. The younger part of our family were present, but my Dear and I found freedom to stay away, having some engagements of importance on hand, which could scarcely be conducted without my attention and direction.

4th Day, 4th.—This day engaged with some improvements about my dwelling, which go on with a prospect of success, tho' the care and expense is considerable. Fine growing weather. The grain, 'tis said, looks promising, and there is a good prospect for fruit.

5th Day, 5th.—Engaged about building my water cistern—five workmen about it—so that I was taken up most of the day. Father and Mother Elliott came up in the morning, and staid 'till evening.

6th Day, 6th.—Cool for the season; clear northerly wind, which was very high and blustering. Was favoured to be pretty well in health.

7th Day, 7th.—Employed to-day in sundry outward concerns. Had some Friends to visit us, and when evening approached could not charge myself with negligence or misspending of precious time.

1st Day, 8th.—At Meeting thrice. All silent as to vocal testimony, which, though uncommon, nevertheless may be all right. Heard of William Savery getting well to Charleston, after a pretty long rough passage.

2d Day, 9th.—This day I was more at leisure than common, though not idle.

3d Day, 10th.—Our Weekly Meeting, and adjournment of Monthly Meeting in course. Rebecca Jones, Samuel Emlen and Thomas Scattergood, all mentioned their intention of going to Long Island Yearly Meeting, and some further.

4th Day, 11*th*.—This day a good deal engaged in some temporal matters. Francis Hopkinson buried to-day. He died suddenly. Had made some bustle in the world, but his life and death proved the words of the wise man to be well founded, *all is vanity and vexation of spirit*, and so it most surely is, independent of Divine approbation in the secret of our own hearts, but that is a sovereign antidote, when well and truly experienced, against all outward evils.

5th Day, 12*th*.—I found my mind easy to stay from Meeting to-day, as it was not the one I properly belong to. In the evening was poorly with the headache, which continued all night very bad.

6th Day, 13*th*.—My headache went off about noon, and I was able to attend to some outward concerns. Our time swiftly passeth away, whether we employ it well or ill. We are instructed to believe it is to be registered, to be hereafter a criterion of acceptance or rejection. O, may we "*give diligence to make our calling and election sure*," "*before we go hence and are seen of men no more.*" I mean you, my dear children, for perhaps few or none but you will be privy to these notes and short observations which I have occasionally penned.

7th Day, 14*th*.—A very soaking rain last night, which in all probability will prove a great blessing to the land, the last two weeks being exceedingly dry and dusty, so that nature languished, that is the vegetable part of it.

1st Day, 15*th*.—At Meeting thrice, where there was good service for Truth. What can we do better, or more for the peace of our minds, than to put ourselves in the way of receiving good, spiritual good, and, if strength is afforded, lift up our hearts to our great Creator and Benefactor in thankfulness for His innumerable blessings. Time is short, and swiftly passeth away. O, my soul, work whilst it is yet day, that so the everlasting night may not overtake thee unprepared.

2*d Day*, 16*th*.—Was much engaged about temporal things, which, tho' necessary to be attended to and prudently conducted, if suffered too much to engross our time and thoughts, do but embarrass and clog the better part, and sway us down to earth and things of no real moment or importance. O, then, for a more lively attention and concern for the one thing needful, and to build beyond the reach of sorrow, pain and disappointment. Went, in the evening, to see a friend.

3*d Day*, 17*th*.—At Meeting in course, John Skyren and Ann Drinker were married. The best wine was at the last; after the Meeting for worship the Preparative Meeting was held. Evening, at Thomas Scattergood's; his children have the small pox. Seymour Hart's grand-child died suddenly. Mary Holton, a young woman, buried.

4*th Day*, 18*th*.—Three months to-day since my dear Aunt Mary Armitt died. A fine, pleasant day, the creation being much benefitted by the late seasonable rains. Johnny went to Joseph Pickering's, in Bucks Co., 30 odd miles, with E. Langdale. I have some prospect of going to New England this Summer.

5*th Day*, 19*th*.—Engaged to-day about paving my yard and completing our water cistern, which we expect will contain 12 or 14 hogsheads. Went to see a friend in the evening.

6th Day, 20*th*.—A fine rain in the night, which continued part of the forenoon, a blessing to the land, producing food for man and the creatures placed under his superintendence. I have my hands full of employment of one kind or another, but 'tis better to be so than idle, for the idle are frequently a burthen to themselves and others, and oftentimes do but little good to their neighbours or those they are intimately connected with.

7th Day, 21*st*.—Continued engaged about secular affairs, and find, as heretofore, that when they are permitted to engross too much of our time they choke the precious seed, and divert the mind from things of the greatest importance; let us, then, watch the door of the heart. Am favoured with tolerable health, for which I desire to be truly thankful, knowing it to be one of the greatest blessings.

1*st Day*, 22*d*.—Had the headache most of the day, tho' I attended Meetings, which were satisfactory and to my comfort.

2*d Day*, 23*d*.—This day employed in various concerns that occurred.

3*d Day*, 24*th*.—At our Monthly Meeting to-day I acquainted Friends that I found my mind drawn to accompany my beloved friend Thomas Scattergood on his religious visit to New England, with which the Meeting concurred, and a minute was directed on the occasion. In the evening, with my dear wife, visited brother Joshua and family.

4th Day, 25th.—My wife's ancient parents spent the day with us. They are exceedingly feeble, but I hope preserved in a good degree of fitness for a removal to a better state when it may please the Great Disposer of events to call them from the troubles of time, having been, for a length of years, circumspect and exemplary in life and conversation. Had a spell of my old complaint.

5th Day, 26th.—This day I had my hair cut off, in hope of its proving beneficial to the disorder I have so long laboured under, and suffered so much pain and misery from, night and day, for thirty or more years.

6th Day, 27th.—This day was occupied in part preparing for my journey to New England, and another part in entertaining several Friends who visited us on account of my intention of going from home for a few months.

7th Day, 28th.—A fine morning, nature in full lustre. The creation may be said to be now in her best robe, the blessing of the Great Creator being evidently over His works, which calls for thankfulness, for who can count the number of mercies bestowed?

I now begin with my Journey to New England.

MY JOURNEY
TO
NEW ENGLAND.

1st Day, 5th Mo., 29th, 1791.

After attending the morning Meeting at our North Meeting House, left my own habitation half after one, in company with my beloved friend and Cousin, Thomas Scattergood, who intends for New England in Truth's service. Got to Burlington about six, to a Meeting appointed for the inhabitants of that place, which proved a favoured opportunity, much seasonable exhortation and counsel being communicated in a good degree of Gospel authority, and I trust the labour bestowed may prove beneficial to some present. The Meeting concluded with prayer. Visited a sick person in the evening. Lodged at John Hoskins' and was favoured to feel pretty well in health.

2d Day, *30th*.—Rose about 4, and after breaking our fast, set out about 6. Called to see a widow woman, who was supposed to be near her end. My companion was favoured with a word of consolation suitable to her low condition of mind and body.— Reached John Wright's, at Crosswick's, about 10, and sat the Quarterly Meeting at Chesterfield, which concluded about 4. After dining went in the evening to Jacob Middleton's, in whose family we had an evening sitting with divers Friends who were present to good satisfaction. From hence I had an opportunity to write to my dear wife.

3d Day, 31*st*.—This was the Youth's Meeting day at Crosswick's, in which my beloved friend and kinsman was largely drawn forth to a large audience, consisting of a mixed multitude, and I trust his fervent labour will be profitable to the encouragement of many seeking religious minds who were present, and came, some of them, from a considerable distance.— After the conclusion of this Meeting, we set out and rode, in a heavy rain, to Benjamin Clark's, at Stony Brook, about 12 miles. We were much wet, but were favoured, so that we did not take much cold.

4th Day, 1*st of Sixth month*.—About 6 we set off, in a drizzly morning, for Rahway, 35 miles. Got to Brunswick about 12, where we dined, and afterwards proceeded on our journey, and arrived at our quarters at Joseph Shotwell's, about 7 in the evening. Our horse performed well, tho' the roads were very heavy, owing to the heavy rain of the preceding day. Had a sitting in the family in the evening.

5th Day, 2*d*.—Morning was foggy and but little wind, yet cleared away about 8. My companion concluded to stay the Week-day Meeting here at Rahway, which was a comfortable time, his testimony being consolatory to the sincere in heart, as well as cautionary to the negligent. After we had dined at Joseph Shotwell's, he accompanied us to Elizabeth

Town Point. The boat got under way about 4, and we had a rough passage over the Bay about 15 miles to New York, where we arrived about 7, and took up our quarters at James Parson's, in Queen Street.

6th Day, 3*d*.—Walked around part of the city, which is much improved since I was here last. Called in to see several Friends. About noon some Friends returned from the Yearly Meeting on Long Island, which has just concluded, our European women Friends Mary Ridgway and Jane Watson being of the number. Afternoon was at Thomas Dobson's, but he being on Long Island, we staid tea with his daughter Peggy, who is lately married to Isaac Sharpless. Afterwards called in to see the family of John Dean, where Cousin Thomas was enabled to impart some suitable counsel to his wife and some of their children present, who have of later years been largely exercised in the school of affliction. We also paid a short visit to Richard Lawrence's daughter, lately married, and removed to this place from Shrewsbury.

7th Day, 4*th*.—Much rain in the night, which continued 'till break of day. After it held up, went on board Captain Layton's vessel, and engaged our passages to Newport. Dined, by invitation, at William Shotwell's, with the European and other Friends. About noon men Friends from the Yearly Meeting at Westbury came to town. Afternoon was employed in getting our horse and chaise on board, in order to be ready for sailing in the morning. We got our horse on board late in the evening; they hoisted him up in slings, and lowered him into the hold with two others, without difficulty or danger. Delivered R. Jones a letter I brought from Philadelphia, and spent part of the evening at Edmund Prior's.

1*st Day*, 5*th*.—A clear cool morning. Forenoon Meeting silent, which was somewhat remarkable, so many public ministers being present. Dined at James Parson's. Afternoon Meeting, Mary Ridgway appeared on the subject of carrying so much earth about us. Advised to disincumber ourselves as fast as possible, that we might be enabled to make some advances in our spiritual journey. Tea at our lodgings. Several Friends kindly came to see us. In the evening was engaged in some necessary matters preparatory to our little voyage to-morrow.

2*d Day*, 6*th*.—Took breakfast early. About 7 went on board Captain Layton's vessel. Jas. Bringhurst, with his wife and son Edward, were our fellow-passengers. Went through a narrow passage commonly called Hell Gate, about 10, safe and well, tho' the wind was a good deal ahead. Passed many handsome seats on the two shores of Long and York Islands. About one, began to open what is called the Sound, between Long Island and the mainland. Was not sick so far, and found some appetite to dinner. Passed by to-day—Hell Gate, Frog's Point, Stony Point, City Island, Cow Bay, Hempsted Harbour, (here the land looks like gardens by the river side,) Matinicock Point, Oyster Bay, Lloyd's Neck, Eden's Neck, and then New Haven on the Connecticut shore. Made pretty good way in the night, tho' the wind was not very favourable; run about 40 miles, so that we were abreast of Negro Point when the sun rose—this Point is reckoned half way between New York and

Newport. I did not get much sleep, tho' on the whole, felt pretty comfortable. Our Captain stood the deck through the night, being a careful experienced man.

3d Day, *7th*—About 10 A. M. the wind fell, and the tide being against us, our Captain came to, and we lay at anchor 'till 1 o'clock. Several vessels passed us bound for New York. Getting under way again, we passed Oyster Pond Point, and came in sight of Plum Island; here Connecticut River opens into the Sound: on which river is Saybrook, and further on is Lyme, a sea-port. As we advanced we passed by the light-house at the entrance of New London Harbour, then Groton and Stonington—towns in Connecticut State. On the right hand we passed by Gull Island, and then entered what is called the Horse Race, from an extraordinary swift tide, which here runs rapidly. Afterwards we went by Gardner's and Fisher's Islands. Block Island is here just discernible.

After a run of 35 miles from Fisher's Island, we came abreast of Point Judith, which is rocky, and sometimes dangerous in stormy seasons. Montauk Point, the East end of Long Island, here terminates, after which appears the open ocean. A number of boats were out hereabouts fishing for mackerel; we caught a couple, which served us for supper. About 10 we turned into our berths, and near 1, all being quiet, I went out upon deck, and found we were safe at anchor in Newport Harbour. In a few minutes Captain Cahoon's vessel, on board of which were our Women Friends and many other passengers, passed by and hailed us, and ran in to the wharf at Newport.

4th Day, 8th.—At break of day our Captain hauled up his anchor, and came alongside the wharf. Soon after Benjamin Hadwen came and invited us to his father, John Hadwen's, house, where we went.— Thomas Robinson and his son met us by the way, and invited us to his home. We soon got our horse and chaise on shore, and then dined on fish which are here very plenty and good. After dinner walked out in the town, which, we were informed, contained about 7,000 inhabitants. Drank tea at Thomas Robinson's, with the European Friends and others. In the evening wrote a letter to my dear wife, to go by the packet to-morrow.

5th Day, 9th.—After a good night's rest—not having had my clothes off the two preceding nights— about 9, rode to Portsmouth, 8 miles, where the Yearly Meeting begins to-day. This was the most pleasant ride we have had since we left home, the road being very good, and the prospect, both going and returning, extensive and diversified with land and water—high ridges of the main-land, and an open view of the ocean and a number of islands. The fields, enclosed with stone fences, looked like gardens, with grain and grass in high vigour.

The Meeting was large—full as many as the house could contain. Many Friends attend it from great distances. Dined at Sampson Shearman's, who has eleven children, six of them daughters nearly grown up, and promise fair to make good wives. Returned to our quarters at Newport in the evening. Afterwards went to see Dorcas Earl's and Captain Layton's families, and after dark had a comfortable sitting a our lodgings, in which Cousin Thomas appeared with encouraging matter to some states present, and Sarah Lundy prayed with great fervency. My companion also was concerned in testimony at Portsmouth, in the forenoon.

6th Day, 1*0th.*—The air moderate, and pleasant for the season; rested well in the night. About sixteen Friends are accommodated with lodgings at Friend Hadwen's; Sarah Lundy, one of them, who purposes to visit Nova Scotia before she returns to her own habitation.

At 11 the Meeting for Worship began, at which appeared Mehetabel Jenkins first, then Sarah Lundy, Jane Watson, and Mary Ridgway—the latter also in supplication. The opportunity was solid and weighty, and I believe the power of Truth generally operated so as to suppress and keep down any improper or unbecoming behaviour in a mixed gathering, supposed to be 1800.

Dined at Thomas Robinson's, took a dish of tea at Captain Layton's, and in the evening had a comfortable sitting at our quarters, where T. S. appeared in testimony, and S. Lundy in prayer, to the satisfaction and strengthening of most or all who were present.

7th Day, 11*th.*—A fine morning. Walked to the pasture to see our horse, and find he fares well—in clover up to his eyes. Attended the Meeting for business in the morning, and dined at Elizabeth Huntington's, (Ruth Bringhurst's sister).

Afternoon was present at a committee of the Yearly Meeting. Drank tea at John Earl's, where we had a sitting, in which Patience Brayton and Mehetabel Jenkins had something comfortable to offer to the sincere in heart present. In the evening there were upwards of 40 Friends at our lodgings.

1st Day, 12*th*.—A pleasant morning. Sarah Lundy attended Portsmouth Meeting. At Newport, Thos. Scattergood, Jane Watson and Mary Ridgway appeared in testimony, all with good authority, to a crowded audience, many of them not of our community, who, I believe, were well satisfied. Dined with the European Friends and others, at Captain Layton's.

Afternoon Meeting, Mary Ridgway, Saml. Emlen and Thomas Scattergood had the service, all with clearness and propriety. Some thought there were not much less than 2000 present, tho' not more than one-half Friends.

At tea at David Williams' who with his wife, a daughter of John Dockra, are a promising young couple. Went afterwards to Thomas Robinson's at the Point, and received a share of the good which was dispensing in a family sitting when we went in. When it concluded, returned to our lodgings, and had another evening sitting, in which T. S. and S. Lundy both appeared.

This day received my dear wife's letter of the 6th inst., which was truly acceptable and satisfactory. Captain Earl arrived to-day, to the rejoicing of his family. Retired to rest about 10, and slept well 'till the day dawned.

2*d Day*, 13*th*—The weather continues fine.— Took breakfast at Ann Carpenter's. She has three daughters, all promising young people, and appears to live comfortably; is a meek-spirited agreeable Friend, who thro' tribulation of various kinds, I hope, will be favoured to reach the Port of Rest in due time, as she holds her integrity to the end.

3d Day, 14*th*.—Meeting did not sit 'till 2 to-day, to give time to the committee to do their business. Dined at Captain Earl's, and called to see his married daughter, wife of Obadiah Williams, who appears to be well settled; her husband is a saddler.

The last sitting of the Yearly Meeting was held this day, and the business concluded about 6 in the evening, and my companion and myself, with other strangers present, had our testimonials endorsed.— Drank tea at Giles Honer's, who, I soon discovered, was an Englishman, but had been many years in this country. He was an intimate acquaintance of John Hadwen, being both from Old England.

Had a solid evening sitting at our lodgings— about thirty present. T. S. was large and satisfactory; S. Lundy was concerned in supplication. Retired to rest about 11, and slept well.

4th Day, 15*th*.—This day wrote to my dear wife, by Edward Bringhurst, who purposes to sail this evening. Many Friends going out of town.

Called to-day to see Hetty Ellery, who confirmed the idea I had long entertained, that those who turn their backs on the Truth in which they have been educated cannot be in possession of true happiness, which can only be attained to by a steady attention and obedience to the dictates of pure wisdom in the secret of our own minds: for however worldly advantages may be possessed and enjoyed, there will be a worm at the bottom of the gourd, which finally will destroy its pleasant shade and comfort.

Dined at my lodgings, on fish—this place of Newport being generally allowed to be the best market for that article in North America.

I have now been eight days in Newport, and had an opportunity of seeing and being conversant among Friends who are universally courteous and respectful, particularly Friend Hadwen's family where we make our home, who, with his good wife and most of the children, are remarkable for that courteous demeanor which, when joined to good understanding, seldom or never fails to gain love and general approbation.

In the afternoon, took a little ride with Peggy Hadwen to a place which goes by the name of Purgatory, being a large rock, split or separated by some great concussion in nature perhaps, as the chasm appears evidently to have been once united. The space or separation appears to be 6 or 8 feet wide, and 20 or 30 feet deep, to the level of the water below, which in stormy times dashes in with great violence.

Here is an open view of the sea, and in going to this part of the island I passed by the place where my dear wife, about 28 years ago, went into the salt water, in hopes of its being beneficial to her health.

This evening we had a sitting in the family, when our friend T. Scattergood had a word of encouragement to the well-minded.

5th Day, 16*th*.—This was Newport Week-day Meeting, at which our European Women Friends were present. Mary Ridgway was engaged in testimony, in which she had to mention the great exercise of her mind since she came to this place, and the prospect she had of a heavy cloud which hung over this island. What it contained she had not yet been favoured to discover, but to her spiritual eye it appeared very black and dark, and she had a sense given her that in the end it would burst on some of the inhabitants of this land, and its effects would be equally dreadful with the fire and brimstone which was anciently by the Lord rained down upon the people of Sodom; and her desire was that the professors of the blessed Truth amongst us might seek in time to Him whose Name and Power only could prove a refuge from the storm, and an invincible defence in every exigency and danger, concluding with something consolatory to the upright and sincere in heart, who should witness preservation under the wing of Everlasting Mercy and Love.

Dined at our lodgings, with many other Friends, after which Mary Ridgway was concerned in a family sitting to speak to the states of divers present with the voice of consolation and encouragement. Latter part of the afternoon went with Peggy Hadwen to see Gould Marsh and family. The evening was spent at home, pleasant and cheerful, yet I trust innocent.

6th Day, 17*th*.—After breakfast my companion and self, with the European and many other Friends, went over to Connanicut, about 3 miles, to an appointed Meeting. This island is fruitful and pleasant, about 9 miles long and 1 broad. We passed by several smaller ones in going over. The Meeting was comfortable and satisfactory. Mary Ridgway and Jane Watson had the principal service.

Mary's testimony was adapted to the state of the audience, who appeared to be a sober and well inclined people, who had not many opportunities of religious instruction. They were affectionately recommended to the Word nigh in the heart, which is sufficient to lead its faithful followers into all Truth, as it is diligently obeyed.

We dined at Joseph Green's, near the ferry, about 30 or more of us, and were kindly entertained. His son married John Earl's daughter. We returned to Newport in the evening, and were wet with a fine shower, which 'tis likely may prove beneficial to the thirsty land which languished for refreshment.

After I returned, wrote a long letter to my son Caleb by Edward Bringhurst, who has been some days detained, by reason of the wind being ahead. Had something of the headache in the evening, and went to bed early, and after a painful night was favoured to be pretty comfortable when the day broke; and so I rose early, which I found to be refreshing to my outward frame and strengthening to my mind.

7th Day, 18*th.*—This day we had no Meeting; my companion went to see some of the children of affliction. Dined at home on black-fish and plaice—both very good fish—which article the inhabitants of Newport are supplied with, both plenty and cheap, all the year round.

Afternoon, took a ride with Peggy and Dorcas Hadwen and Sally Dennis, to Samuel Elam's place or farm, about 5 miles from town, where we took tea. His house is in elegant style. Walked around his garden, and some part of his land near the shore, and saw a large button-wood tree, which they said measured six yards around the body. Had a delightful ride home, where we arrived in the close of the evening.

1st Day, 19*th*.—At morning Meeting our friend Hugh Judge, from Wilmington, in the Delaware State, who has been in those parts about 15 months or more, was engaged in testimony and prayer. Dined at Giles Honer's. The afternoon Meeting was silent, but satisfactory. Walked to our quarters in a fine rain, which will doubtless do much good in the vegetable kingdom, now in its pride.

After tea had a sitting in the family, when my companion was concerned to exercise his ministerial gift, and was engaged to speak to the aged and also to the youth present, by way of encouragement and comfort. Divers Friends called in to see us in the evening, which passed in pleasant conversation, and we retired to rest a little after 10, with a view of leaving this place to-morrow morning.

Two inhabitants of this town were interred to-day. From what I have experienced in respect to the weather so far, I judge it to be several degrees cooler on this island than at my native place. The air from the sea surrounding it makes it full a garment cooler, and very pleasant and healthy, so that in the heat of Summer here is a great resort of strangers from the Southern parts of the continent.

2*d Day*, 20*th*.—My companion being easy to leave Newport, we set off about 9, and crossed the river which separates Rhode Island from the main-land, at Fogland's Ferry, to which Barney and Dorcas Hadwen bore us company. We had but an unfavourable passage over, being about a mile wide.

Soon after we landed, we dined at a friendly man's house, where my companion was exercised in his gift, just before we set off, to about half a dozen sober persons who were present, and not of our Society.

We then put forward for Bedford, by the lower road over Hicks' Bridge, and riding over 20 miles of the roughest and most stony land I ever saw, reached Abraham Russel's, at Bedford, about 9 at night, where we understood that our Women Friends, with Samuel Emlen, Sarah Lundy, and divers others, had got into William Rotch's a little while before us.

We also were informed that Capt. Parker purposed to sail at the 6th hour in the morning for Nantucket, with whom we concluded to embark. We left our horse and chaise under the care of our kind friend Russel.

This town of Bedford is a little sea-port, and most of the inhabitants are concerned in the fishing trade—particularly those of the Rotch family, who carry on a considerable trade from this place, and are concerned in the spermaceti works here.

3d Day, 21*st*.—This is called the longest day in the year, and proved a fine agreeable morning. Tho' the wind was not sufficient to promise a speedy passage over to Nantucket, yet we put off about the time appointed, but were 'till towards 11 without making much way ahead; however, the wind then freshened, and we sailed at the rate of 5 knots an hour. Later in the afternoon the wind increased, and we run 7 or 8 knots, and passed Wood's Hole and Martha's Vineyard, and so into the main ocean. About 5 o'clock had sight of the wind-mills on Nantucket.

Out of about 25 passengers, about 4 were sea-sick, and those not to any great degree. For my own part, I had a good appetite, and felt pretty comfortable, and as I apprehended a spell of sea-sickness would not hurt me, expressed my willingness to have taken our friend Jane Watson's share, if it could have been transferred.

At sunset we were within about 2 miles of Sherburn, the principal town on Nantucket, where we landed about 8 o'clock. This place contains about 500 houses, built generally of timber, and 4,500 inhabitants, chiefly Friends. They are mostly employed in the fisheries and other branches of business which depend thereon. There are about eight or nine spermaceti works in the town and on the island; five or six hundred head of cows and cattle, two or three hundred horses, and about seven thousand sheep—the latter kept as common property, and run at large on the island, there being but little fencing. This and the preceding day was their time of shearing, at which there is a kind of festival.

We took up our quarters at Samuel Rodman's, (who married William Rotch's daughter,) which is one of the principal houses for entertaining Friends on the island. Wm. Rotch, Jr. and Thomas Rotch each married a sister of Samuel Rodman, and are both settled at Bedford; so also is Thomas Hazard, whose wife is another sister. They are all concerned in business together, as I understood, that is the fishery, having a number of vessels in the trade.

At S. Rodman's also lodged M. Ridgway, J. Watson, S. Emlen, S. Lundy, E. Martin, and Wm. Rotch (the younger), besides ourselves and some others. This island is called about 12 miles long, and 3 or 4 broad; and they raise indian corn, rye and oats, and a variety of garden produce. Our passage occupied 13 hours.

4th Day, 22*d*.—Having had a comfortable night's rest after our little voyage, rose between 4 and 5, and after breakfast went in to see Sarah Barney, who lives a few doors from our lodgings; then called in at Josiah Barker's; afterwards at Wm. Brown's, where we had a sitting—T. S. and S. E. being in company, who both had something to communicate—then came home and dined at a table plentifully spread.

After dinner visited Jethro Mitchel, and called in to see a new house built by Peter Folger, which has a flat roof, as have several others in this place, which they say answers well.

Towards evening came home, and felt a good deal weary with our walk through the sandy streets of Sherburn,—tho' I judge the heat is more moderate than in our city at this season, the mercury standing at about 66 degrees. In the evening it rained a little, which brought our other lodgers home, when we had a solid sitting together in silence, and afterwards spent the evening together in agreeable conversation.

5th Day, 23*d*.—This was Week-day Meeting in course, which began at 11, and was a large gathering. Jane Watson and Samuel Emlen had the principal service. A Preparative Meeting was also held, which sat long.

After dinner, walked out into the town, and returned towards evening, when the neighbours coming in, there was a family sitting. Jane Watson and Mary Ridgway appeared in testimony, and Thomas Scattergood in prayer, all to our comfort and encouragement in well-doing.

6th Day, 24th.—A foggy morning, which is not uncommon here, but as it comes off the sea, they are not reckoned unwholesome. We dined to-day, by invitation, at Josiah Bartlett's, with many other Friends. Our European Friends were not of the number, on account of some indisposition.

Afternoon, in company with William Rotch and two other Friends, took a ride out on the island, which is level for the most part, and a light sandy soil. Observed their indian corn, rye and oats to be very light; I think the probable produce (in our country,) would not be accounted more than a quarter of a crop.

We went to a fishing town called Siasconset, about 8 miles from Sherburn, which contained about 20 comfortable houses, but had but one or two families in them at present, being not the time for taking fish. We returned to our quarters in the evening, and had a good night's rest.

7th Day, 25th.—A foggy morning; cleared away about 10, when we went to their Monthly Meeting, which was large—there being about 300 families of Friends on the island. J. Watson, M. Ridgway, S. E. and T. S. all had some service, and, with an adjourned sitting in the afternoon, it did not conclude 'till near dark, tho' they had a good clerk, and the business, I thought, was well-conducted.

In the evening divers Friends arrived from the main-land, with a view of attending the Quarterly Meeting now coming on, which goes by the name of Sandwich, and is held here once in the year.

1st Day, 26*th*.—It is thought about forty or fifty Friends have arrived from distant parts to attend the Quarterly Meeting. This day M. R. and J. Watson were both poorly, and did not get to Meeting; however, we were favoured with a satisfactory one.

Forenoon, Samuel Emlen and Thomas Scattergood were both engaged in religious labour; Sarah Lundy appeared in prayer. The Meeting was large, and a great proportion were young people, more women than men, the latter being (many of them) out at sea. The testimonies delivered were close and searching, tho' on the whole encouraging. Afternoon, my companion was also concerned in a public way.

In the evening there was a comfortable sitting at our lodgings. T. S., J. W., S. E., and M. R. were large in testimony, and my companion T. S. also appeared in supplication. The scope and tendency of what was delivered, was, to encourage to diligence and faithfulness in pursuing the right road to future happiness; to work whilst the day of visitation was lengthened out, and not to withdraw from manifested duty, lest we should incur Divine displeasure, as time was short, and the business of it of the greatest consequence and importance.

2d Day, 27*th*.—We took a ride a little way in the country this morning—had a view of the sea and lighthouse—after which we returned and dined at William Hussey's. Took a dish of tea at Jethro Mitchel's, and then called to see Peter Barney. In the evening was not very well, and had but a poor night. Wrote to my dear wife.

3d Day, 28*th*.—This day the Quarterly Meeting for business was held, which continued, by adjournment, in the afternoon. Dined at our lodgings. The last sitting continued 'till dusk. When we came home were much worn down und fatigued.

4th Day, 29*th*.—Breakfasted at the widow Barker's. Afterwards went home and wrote a long piece, with an intention of putting it into my collection when I get to my home in Philadelphia: it is on the subject of the Excellency of the Christian Religion. Dined at Sarah Barney's, with our good Women and several other Friends. Afternoon, wrote to my dear wife.

5th Day, 30*th*.—Had some thoughts to-day about crossing over to Bedford, but it was finally concluded, chiefly on Mary Ridgway's account, to defer going to another day, especially as the wind is not altogether fair. So we went to the usual Week-day Meeting, where Mary Mitchel, Jane Watson, and Mary Ridgway were engaged in testimony and prayer. It was a solid favoured time. Dined at Samuel Rodman's. After dinner went to inquire for an opportunity of forwarding a letter I wrote in the morning to my son Johnny, and one to my wife, which I forwarded by Capt. Wing for New York.

6th Day, 1*st of Seventh month*.—The wind being still contrary, prevented any of our company from crossing over to the main. In the morning several of us (M. R. and J. Watson of the number,) rode out a few miles to the sea-shore, and after a pleasant airing of 7 or 8 miles, returned home and dined; after which S. Emlen and some others went out of town in two chaises, and returned in the evening.

I employed myself in transcribing a piece of writing, which I finished in the evening. After dark, a family sitting took place, when T. S. and J. W. were concerned in a word of exhortation, and after some pleasant improving conversation, we retired to our rest, and were favoured with a good night.

7th Day, 2d.—This morning dawned and afforded a favourable wind, which several of our company will make use of to return to Bedford, about sixty miles. About 10, Capt. Parker in the packet left the wharf, with 25 passengers, but my companion and Samuel Emlen concluded to stay over First-day, that is to-morrow, and wait 'till next trip, which probably may be the beginning of the week. We had a favoured parting Meeting at Saml. Rodman's, when a number of Friends accompanied our European visitors and divers others, on board, there being a good prospect of a favourable run over to the place of destination.

Dined with several Friends at Jethro Mitchel's; afterwards called to see Jonathan Jenkins, and then took a ride about three miles with S. Rodman and his wife and five children, to see some of the indian natives, a very few of whom yet remain on the island, where they were formerly very numerous; and there are still, at a neighbouring island called Martha's Vineyard, about one hundred and fifty, who make out to live pretty comfortably, having a tract of land secured to them and their posterity by the government of Massachusetts.

1*st Day*, 3*d*.—A cool day, the wind being in the Eastern board. At morning Meeting Mary Mitchel and Samuel Emlen had the service; afternoon, Thos. Scattergood, S. Emlen and Mary Mitchel. Drank tea at William Brown's. Came home at dusk, and found them sitting in silence. After we came in, T. S. and S. E. had a word of exhortation to drop; and so this day ended—I hope not unprofitably.

2*d Day*, 4*th*.—The wind continues Easterly and quite cool. After breakfast, T. S., S. E., and several others of us visited three families, and a portion of good was handed out for their encouragement. Walked down to the wharf, when S. Emlen agreed to embark with Captain Gardner for Newport. About 1 he embarked, and the vessel put off with a fair wind; but my beloved companion does not find himself at liberty to leave this island yet, which was no small cross to us, at least it was particularly so to me, who felt very willing and desirous to be moving a little ahead, so as to have a prospect of finishing our work.

3*d Day*, 5*th*.—Captain Parker returned from Bedford this morning, and reported that our friends who went over with him had a good passage of about nine hours. Dined to-day at George Hussey's, where we had a sitting. We then visited the family of Benj. Worth, where a portion of comfort and encouragement was dispensed. When this concluded we proceeded to Benj. Barney's, where my companion and Sarah Lundy were again furnished with something suitable to communicate.

We then went over to Jethro Mitchel's, and took some refreshments, and so returned to our lodgings in the evening, when divers of the neighbours coming in, further service in a religious way ensued, and S. Lundy concluded in supplication, so that I heard, at the several opportunities this day, six sermons and two prayers. May I profit in proportion to the mercies bestowed.

4th Day, 6th.—Dined to-day at William Macy's, and had tea at William Brown's, where we had a satisfactory sitting in which E. Martin appeared in a short prayer. T. S. and S. Lundy also had a word in season to the exercised traveller, and Sarah Lundy concluded with supplication.

After we came home to our quarters, several Friends dropped in, and falling into silence, Cousin Thomas had a communication of considerable length, and S. L. also, which delayed supper 'till 10, after which went to bed and slept comfortably 'till morning.

Nothing contributes more to true happiness than a peaceful mind—without which, that is to say a good conscience, there most certainly can be no such thing attainable. Let us then, make it our principal object and aim, and relinquish every inferior satisfaction to pursue it alone.

5th Day, 7th.—This was Week-day Meeting, in which Thomas and Sarah had laborious service—the latter concluded the Meeting in prayer. Dined at our kind friend Jethro Mitchel's.

In the afternoon visited Joseph Harris' family, where my companion had service. Then called at Richard Mitchel's and Jonathan Macy's—the last mentioned being a blind Friend and Elder. At all these places our Ministering Friends had employment in their gifts, and I hope to profit, at least to those who make the necessary improvement by the labour in much love bestowed. Evening was spent at our lodgings, as a number of Friends called in, as usual; we were mostly drawn into silence, and there was an addition to the labour of the day. Got to bed about 11, and was favoured with a good rest 'till morning.

6th Day, *8th*.—High Northerly wind, which prevents the packet going over to Bedford, and Captain Worth to Halifax. In the last-mentioned vessel S. Lundy and her companions, Dorcas Brown and Jos. Harris, expect to embark on a religious visit to Friends in Nova Scotia, where some under our name have been driven and dispersed by the convulsions occasioned by the late war.

Dined at Richard Mitchel's, and when we rose from table, a messenger came to acquaint us that Captain Worth was ready to put to sea, the wind having come fair, and he was anxious to make use of it; so we immediately took our departure to Samuel Rodman's. From there we conveyed the Friends' stores down to the packet, and with six or eight Friends went on board the Halifax vessel, which lay without the bar. Got on board about 5 P. M. with some difficulty, there being a large swell. Returned back in the evening, having seen the Friends safe on board and under sail.

Found a vessel just arrived from Philadelphia, but no letters from my family. After dark walked down to the water to take a view of the light-house, which is about 10 miles distant, on a sandy point of this island, and is of great use to the trade in these parts.

7th Day, 9*th*.—My companion was poorly to-day, and kept mostly within doors. Captain Waterman arrived from Philadelphia, but we had no letters. The Friends on their way for Halifax have a fine wind, with pleasant weather. Dined on fresh cod-fish. After dinner, rode out about four miles, in company with S. Rodman, E. Martin and some others; viewed the public corn-field, (about three or four hundred acres in one body,) tho' it appeared pinched with the drouth —the soil being light and sandy. We were shown the place where our friend John Richardson had that memorable meeting, mentioned in his journal in the year 1701.

1st Day, 10*th*.—A fine morning. Wind at S.W. which is fair for our friends bound to Halifax. At Meeting in the forenoon my companion had a favoured time, which afforded considerable ease to his exercised mind. The common First-day Meeting here, I think, is quite equal in numbers to our North Meeting in Philadelphia. The afternoon Meeting was silent, and smaller than that in the morning. After dark had a family sitting, which concluded the day.

2d Day, 11*th*.—My companion, apprehending he should be most easy to have a meeting with some sober people about 6 miles eastward on the island, agreeable to his prospect, one was appointed at the third hour. Several Friends from Sherburn accompanied us, and he had an open satisfactory time among them, and came home relieved. In his way back, he, with some other Friends, called to visit a young woman who had been some time in a declining state of health and thought to be near the solemn close.

In the evening a number of Friends came to our lodgings, and after sitting some time in silence Cousin Thomas had a word of encouragement to the well-minded; and so this day finished.

3d Day, 12*th*.—A pleasant morning, with the wind at S. W. Wrote several letters to-day. Afternoon, took a walk to a part of the town I had not before been in. Drank tea at Sylvanus Macy's. In the evening divers friends called to see us, and after sitting awhile in silence, without any verbal communication, we parted, and at the usual time retired to our chamber, and rested 'till the dawn of another day.

4th Day, 13*th*.—This day we went on board the packet with Captain Parker, with a fair wind for Bedford—our company, Samuel Rodman and wife, our kind hosts, Hannah Rodman, his sister, Wm. Shotwell, Elizabeth Martin, Cousin Thomas Scattergood, and myself. The freshness of the wind made some of us, especially our women, a good deal sick.

We arrived at Bedford in about 9 hours, and found our friends Mary Ridgway and Jane Watson at Wm. Rotch's, just returned from visiting some Meetings in the neighbourhood between Providence and that place.

Here we heard of the decease of Job Scott's wife, (a heavy stroke to him,) having left behind her six small children, and not in affluent circumstances. In the evening went up to Abraham Russel's, where we lodged. Our horse was in good order, having been well taken care of during the three weeks we had been on Nantucket.

5th Day, 14*th*.—Was favoured to be pretty well after the fatigue of yesterday's passage, and thankful we had got to the main-land again. Attended the Week-day Meeting at Bedford, where my companion had acceptable service. Dined at W. Rotch's. Afterwards went to view the shipping and town, and returned to our lodgings early, in order to write to my family.

6th Day, 15th.—This morning finished three letters, which I committed to the care of Cousin Lizzie Martin, who is returning home to Rahway. She set off this morning about 8, after which we went to Long Plain Meeting, about 9 miles. M. Ridgway, Jane Watson, and my companion had acceptable service therein. Dined at a Friends' House, near the Meeting. Afterwards came back to Bedford in good time in the evening.

7th Day, 16th.—There being no public Meeting to-day, we went round to visit our friends—as Caleb Green's, Barnabas Russel's, Thos. and Wm. Rotch's —where we dined with the European Friends and other Friends. Took tea at T. Rotch's, and had a sitting afterwards. Here our friend J. W. mentioned the common saying that "prevention is better than cure," and applied it in a spiritual sense, with that fitness that I hope may have some good effect, if we practice what she so well recommended—that was, obedience to Divine requirings early, and so prevent the long train of evils which result from a departure from the law of the Lord, written and unfolded in the secret of our own minds from day to day, which will produce that best of treasures, peace to the soul when our race in this world is finally ended.

1st Day, 17th.—Attended Meeting at Bedford, which I thought was made up of between three and four hundred persons, many of them not members of our Society. Cousin Thomas Scattergood had the principal service in a doctrinal way. J. W. followed him, and then he appeared in supplication. So the morning sitting ended—I think, well. Dined at Barnabas Russel's, who has a large flock of children.

Afternoon Meeting, T. S. was first concerned in testimony, and M. R. made an addition to various states present, which, we understood afterwards was fitly spoken, there being several seeking persons from different parts at the Meeting.

When it concluded, we called in to see Joseph Austin and James Davis, Timothy's brother, who is in |the ministry, and well approved. At both these places Thomas dropped some tender counsel. Drank tea at Thos. Hazard's, after which had a sitting with about 25 Friends at William Rotch's, where all our Ministering Friends were engaged in testimony, after which we returned to our lodgings at Abraham Russel's.

2d Day, 18*th*.—This morning early, Mary and Jane, S. Rodman and wife, Jesse Coupland, and another Friend or two, set off for Falmouth, about 40 miles, in order to be at an appointed Meeting there on Third Day. My companion and I also got on the road about 9, to attend Aponiganset Monthly Meeting. Thomas was largely drawn forth to a large audience, in a close searching testimony, yet with caution not to hurt the tender, precious life in any humble sincere hearts; some such, we had reason to hope, were present. The Meeting continued from 11 'till 6, and was wearisome to the body.

Called at a Friend's house about half a mile from the Meeting House, and took some refreshment.— Then went to Wm. Rotch's at Bedford, and drank tea, and took our leave of his and several other families, intending for Sandwich to-morrow. Came home to our lodgings after dark, and retired to rest.

3d Day, 19*th*.—Left a letter for my dear wife with Sally Russel, and, it being a most lovely morning, set off for Sandwich about 7, and in about 8 or 9 miles riding got off the stones, and into the other extreme among the sands, which was as heavy and difficult for the horse in our heavy chaise.

The land in this day's ride was very poor, so that we pitied the inhabitants who had to get their living out of such a barren soil. However, I have frequently made this remark, that those indigent people who have, from one generation to another, been accustomed to such a scant subsistence, seldom lay it much to heart, but endure the ills of life with full as much fortitude, and with less complaint or repining, than those in a higher sphere; for happiness consists very much in a contentment and resignation to our lot, and nature being easily reconciled to small things, food, clothes, and fire are all that the opulent can enjoy, and the very great fullness which some rest in often produces cares, anxieties, vexations, and disappointments which the poor are in a great measure exempt from. In our passage through the wilderness of this world there is but one object which ought to engage our principal pursuit and attention, that is, the securing a better inheritance in a future state, where sorrow, pain and grief cannot invade or annoy.

Dined at Israel Fearing's, a poor inn, and fed our horses—Joseph Austin and Abraham Smith kindly bearing us company. Set off about 3, and reached Paul Wing's about 7, where we lodged.

4th Day, 20*th*.—In the morning, after breakfast, my companion was disposed to have the family, consisting of 9 children besides others of the family, together, and he had something suitable to drop amongst them; and we left them in a loving tender frame, and rode a few miles to Joseph Wing's, where we left our horses, and walked to Sandwich Meeting through the rain, where Cousin Thomas, Jane, and Mary all appeared in testimony.

After we had dined, went forward about 11 miles through the wet, to John Wing's, where we were well accommodated, and rising early on

5th Day, 21*st*, set out about 5, in order to attend Yarmouth Meeting, about 15 miles, which we rode in a heavy rain, and reached the appointed Meeting there about the usual time of gathering. They were but a small company of about 40 persons, and very raw and undisciplined. However, there was a portion meted out by all our Ministering Friends, which would, if properly applied and improved, prove wholesome nourishment, and tend to invigorate and strengthen their spiritual senses and faculties. But what can we say or do for those who are dead, and even buried, as to any sense or savour of the Divine quickening, animating life proceeding from the Fountain of all Fulness? In short, nothing less than the power and efficacy of His tremendous judgment can ever awaken those who are as it were dead in trespasses and sins.

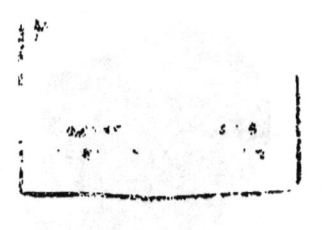

Mary Ridgeway
Of Mount Mellick, Queen's Co. Ireland
Visited America 1791. –

M. A. Ag° 67.

Cousin Thomas had an opportunity in the family where we dined, after the other Friends had set off, but we overtook them after riding 7 or 9 miles, and all returned together to John Wing's, where we had a sitting in the evening. T. S. had a word of encouragement to some present, after which we retired to our chambers, being a good deal fatigued with 30 miles of riding, through the rain mostly.

This is in general a poor part of the Massachusetts State, except here and there some spots of tolerable land, supported in great measure by salt marsh, which in some places are extensive. Barnstable—which we passed through—is a pretty noted town, and produces abundance of onions, which are cultivated to advantage. Further down on the peninsula of Cape Cod, which runs perhaps 40 miles further out into the ocean, the land is so poor that the Government has not only exempted the inhabitants from taxation, but allowed them a bounty for continuing to carry on the fishery, which is the principal support of the settlers hereaway.

6th Day, 22*d*.—The weather proving fair this morning, after breakfast, and a sitting in our Friend John Wing's family—in which Mary Ridgway and Jane Watson were led to speak with great plainness and in a close manner to the head of the family—we proceeded on our way to Sandwich, and when we came near to that place my companion expressed that his mind was easy to go on towards Boston. So we stopped at Joseph Wing's, and took our leave of our Women Friends, and his family, and went on about 12 o'clock, with Aaron Wing as a pilot.

Dined at Ellis' Tavern by the sea-side; so put forward, and it proved warm and sultry going through the woods in such sandy roads as we found hereabouts. We were obliged to go moderately, and therefore did not reach Plymouth 'till near 7.

This is the place where the first settlers in New England landed, I think, about the year 1632. It is now a town of about 200 houses, the people all of the Presbyterian profession; their business, chiefly fishing for cod. They have a good harbour, and conveniences for drying their fish, which is their principal dependence, as the land around the town appears very light and unproductive.

Baiting our horse and refreshing ourselves, we kept on, and after a difficult travel in the dark, came, about 11 at night, to Elizabeth Gould's, at Pembroke, who got up and entertained us kindly, and we rested well 'till morning.

7th Day, 23*d*.—Fair weather. On the road about 6, passing by Pembroke Meeting House, where our European Friends are to be to-morrow. We called at John Bayley's, who kindly put us on our way a few miles, our guide, Aaron Wing, parting with us here.

Passing through Hanover we came to Weymouth; here we dined at an inn, and in the afternoon pursued our way to Boston, (the road being populous and good,) where we arrived about 7, and rode through the main street to our lodging at Griffith Barney's, at New Boston, who received us kindly.

Here we had the pleasure of seeing two of our townsmen, Joseph Richardson and Jonathan Willis, who brought us several letters from our friends in

Philadelphia, which contained a satisfactory account of their welfare.

1st Day, 24*th*.—Attended two Meetings in Boston to-day—at each of which Cousin Thomas had something to communicate, particularly in the afternoon, which concluded with supplication.

There are but few members of our society in Boston—not more than 6 or 7 families—and it seems as if the innocent blood shed in this town about 130 years ago was not yet atoned for; 'tho the present generation are much altered in respect to their conduct towards Friends, as persecution on a religious account hath long since ceased, and they are now even exempt from militia fines, and the support of an hireling ministry and worship houses.

Wrote to my dear wife, by Jos. Richardson, who sets off for Philadelphia to-morrow, in the stage. Dined at Griffith Barney's, and drank tea at Ann Orrick's.

2d Day, 25*th*.—Had my horse shod, and chaise oiled and rubbed up by a coach-maker. Walked out to see the town, in company with Ebenezer Pope—first to Beacon Hill, which commands an extensive view of the town, the harbour, Castle Island, (also many other islands in the bay within 7 or 10 miles,) Gov. Hancock's house, Cambridge town and University, Bunker's Hill, where the bloody battle was fought between the British and Americans in the beginning of the late civil wars. A monument is erected on Beacon Hill, which must have cost a considerable sum, and on it are inscribed the memorable events of the distressing times we have of later years passed through.

We also viewed the Alms-house, Work-house, State House, Faneuil Hall, the Market, Long Wharf, and other public buildings and private dwellings, some of them stately and elegant. The duck manufactory was a pleasing sight, and carried on to good advantage.

Our friend Ebenezer Pope informed me that he had made it a point to be particular in his inquiry, in order to ascertain the place where our Friends William Robinson and Marmaduke Stevenson were put to death, and he thought he could fix the spot within a few rods. The histories of Friends which mention the transaction are not explicit on that head—neither is it very material—yet when one is at Boston it seems quite natural to make some inquiry about it, tho' the inhabitants now show rather an aversion to having the matter revived; and indeed, Christian charity would forbid our making the children answerable for the misconduct of their forefathers, whose deeds they condemn, both in word and conduct. However, there can be nothing criminal in endeavouring to fix the place where the tragedy was executed.

Ebenezer Pope told me several circumstances tending to fix the spot, which he led me to, very nearly. Some of them, for my own satisfaction, I will set down here.

He says, one of our historians mentions a boat, with some sober people, coming from Nantasket, to see the bloody business, who sat therein, while it was performed, in a little creek near the gallows. The entrance of this creek is still visible near Boston Neck, and the remaining ground towards the opposite shore, a little more than a quarter of a mile over, is still low, tho' it has been filled up considerably for building.

He further says that old Friend Bagnel told him of a conversation which he had with an Old Woman at Charleston, who informed him she was about 10 years old when the occurrence happened, and got leave of her parents to go and see the execution, and after crossing Penny Ferry, as it was then called, she ran along the beach until she came in view of the gallows —which, by the present situation of land and water, tends to fix the place somewhere near where our Friend Pope supposed it to be.

Add to this his account of a Public Friend from England, who when here was concerned to make inquiry on the subject, and walking out to the place, and leaning on the fence, after a solemn pause, said, "Here lie my dear Friends: I smell their bones."

Also, a sober neighbour of his, being near the spot during the late troubles, related to him (that is E. Pope,) as follows:—Ruminating in his mind on the judgments which then hung over the land, and being deeply thoughtful and pensive of the cause, was made, as by a secret impulse, to stand still, and a voice as it were run through his mind—*Here lie the innocent Quakers*, and the very spot, or place, seemed pointed out to him in a very particular manner.

All these circumstances unite to render it almost certain that somewhere near the place he showed me, the affecting tragedy was performed.

Bishop tells us that when their lives were taken, they were denied burial, and their naked bodies cast into a hole, and not permitted to be covered; which was soon after overflowed with water, which probably might have been occasioned by the rising of the tide over the low grounds already mentioned.

I speak now of William Robinson and Marmaduke Stevenson, for as to Mary Dyer and William Leddra, Friends were permitted to take away and bury their bodies.

This Friend Pope also related a conversation which lately passed between two of his neighbours—one of them grandson to Edward Rawson, who was Secretary to Governor Endicot, who spake much in favour of the piety of the first settlers, and what godly people they were, compared to the present generation. "Say you so?" said his friend; "I am of a different mind:—so far from thinking them virtuous, good people, I look upon them to have been the veriest devils that ever existed in human shape, and, to be plain with you, your grandfather was no better than the rest of them." "Why, what do you mean, sir?" said his neighbour. "I mean as I say, sir; that so far from being pious and godly, their cruelty and wickedness exceeded all example since the days of the Reformation from Popery. Have you never read the history of the Quakers' sufferings in this country, sir?" No! "Then I will take care to furnish you with a sight of it, and I am persuaded, from your uprightness and candour, you will join with me in utterly condemning the principles and practices of those who first settled in this country; who, fleeing from persecution in their native land, became far before their persecutors in England in point of hard-heartedness and barbarity." So he furnished him with Besse's

History of the Sufferings of our Friends in New England.

After some weeks he called upon him again, and asked if he had read it. He said "Yes." He then queried, "What was his opinion of their ancestors now?" "Why, sir," he replied, "I stand informed of what I never before was acquainted with, and may acknowledge, with the Queen of the South, that the one-half had not been told me. So I am compelled to be of your mind, sir, and allow that they were not the men I apprehended them to be."

This was the substance of their conversation, being two Presbyterians, and it may reasonably be supposed that few of those now upon the stage have much knowledge of the proceedings of those early times against our innocent brethren and sisters, only for bearing their testimony to the Truth; for it has, without doubt, been the earnest endeavour of the writers and leaders amongst them, to mutilate and suppress all accounts which had a tendency to criminate and set in an unfavourable point of view the conduct of their forefathers. But faithful and impartial history will still preserve the truth of those transactions which cast such a shade of infamy upon the high professors of the Christian name in that day.

And something remarkable and memorable it will be, if in future time, in the very midst of the country where the persecution raged the hottest, that is, between Boston and Salem, our Yearly Meeting for New England should be established, and a standard for the Truth, as held by us as a religious society, be erected.

And if the professors under our name were but in the possession of what they hold up to the world, and acted agreeably to the principles we maintain, no doubt there would be a gathering from many of those sects, who are groaning under their heavy task-masters, and ready to say, many seeking religious minds among them, at least, "*Who will show us any good?*" sensibly feeling in the secret of their own minds, a want, which nothing outward can satisfy—a deficiency, which outward worship, service, and ceremonies can not supply.

For, indeed, nothing can satisfy the immortal part but that which is really Divine and spiritual—agreeably to that Scripture testimony, "*God is a spirit, and they that worship Him must worship Him in spirit and in truth,*" that is, all who approach before Him in an acceptable manner.

Our European Women Friends and their company came into Boston in the afternoon, and we were with them at Ann Orrick's 'till towards bed-time, when we retired to our lodgings at Griffith Barney's.

3*d Day*, 26*th*.—A fine cool morning. This day we had an appointed Meeting in Boston, at which our Friend Mary Ridgway appeared first, I thought, under much oppression and exercise, tho' a measure of strength was afforded to go through her service in good authority, to an auditory mostly made up of those who were not of our community. Jane Watson was next concerned, then my companion, and the Meeting concluded with some degree of satisfaction.

Dined at our lodging, with Captain Needham, who brought me three letters from Philadelphia. Set off, in the afternoon, for Lynn, over Charleston and Malden Bridges, lately built, the execution of which do great credit to the spirit and ingenuity of the people hereaway. Reached Lynn in good time, and put up at Samuel Collins'. The Women Friends' quarters were at Sylvanus Hussey's.

4th Day, *27th*.—At Meeting at Lynn, where Jane was first concerned in testimony, Mary next, and my companion had the concluding service; all, I thought, had wisdom and utterance given to divide the Word in fit proportions to various states in a large gathering or assembly, made up mostly of those who profess with us, generally of the middle-aged and younger class, who make a pleasing appearance, tho' if we might judge from the doctrine delivered, there was need for many to endeavour to *live* nearer the Holy Principle, and then they would know where and how to retire, in their silent meetings, to the inexhaustable Fountain of Living Virtue, and know a drawing water from their own wells, some no doubt, would be commissioned to tell to others what the Lord had done for their souls—and be in truth able to direct the sincere seekers to the Fountain of all Fullness—and by example and precept encourage and strengthen the hindermost of the flock in all holy conversation and Godliness becoming the Gospel of Christ.

Dined with many other Friends at Samuel Collins' where we were plentifully entertained. Afternoon, some of our company went to see a young person who had been sick a considerable time.

Samuel Rodman and myself took a 5-mile ride to Marblehead, a town of some note, where the inhabitants are mostly employed in the fishing trade or cod fishery, which is their principal dependence for a support. They told us there were sixty small schooners in that business, belonging to their port, that make several trips yearly to the fishing banks.

We returned about 7 to Samuel Collins' and had a sitting in his family, at which all our Ministering Friends were led to speak, with much precision, to some states present, after which we supped and retired to rest.

5th Day, 28*th*.—We left S. Collins' about the eighth hour, and came to Salem in good Meeting time. Jane took the lead—Mary followed in the power and demonstration. Their fervent labour had an evident effect upon a mixed multitude, among whom were two Parsons, or Ministers so called, also a Member of Congress.

The authority of Mary's testimony seemed to command an assent, tho' evidently with some reluctance, in minds present. However, the Truth will have its own weight, and naturally tends to keep in awe, and at least silence the spirits who have the will but not the power to oppose.

So I hope the labour of this day will not be lost to the sincere-hearted. As to those who hold the Truth by tradition only, and have never known it to cleanse the heart from unrighteousness, they may still beat the air, and true wisdom will neverthless be justified of all her children.

When the Meeting ended, my companion gave notice that he intended to be at that Meeting of Salem that day week following. Dined at James Needham's. I find Salem to be a considerable sea-port town, and accounted next to Boston for trade and population. I went on board a new vessel built by a merchant of the name of Darby, that measured, as they informed us, 600 tons. She is called the Grand Turk, and is intended for the India trade.

I was shown the place where these infatuated New England people, about the year 1692, put 19 persons, men and women, to death, for witchcraft, and pressed one other poor creature to death for the same pretended crime, tho' it afterwards sufficiently appeared that there was very little (if any) just ground for proceeding in this severe manner against them, and some of the foremost of their historians confessed in print that they were under a strong delusion of Satan.

At the time they stopped this persecution there were a great number more in confinement and under accusation, and one of their foremost Priests or Ministers among the rest,—and so they dismissed the poor creatures after the law was repealed.

It was remarkable that none of our Friends were accused; but it was rather by some considered as a judgment upon them for their cruelty in taking the lives of our brethren, William Robinson, Marmaduke Stevenson, Mary Dyer, and William Leddra, and the severe whipping, cutting off ears, banishment, and other barbarous treatment of very many others of our dear Friends, a few years before.

And this was not the only indication of the hand of Heaven being against them, for the native Indians, for a long course of years after they had stained their hands with the blood of our innocent Friends, were, as it were, let loose upon the people of the land, and many hundred were murdered, and carried into captivity and tortured to death in cold blood.

Another remarkable circumstance which took place in this Government of Massachusetts Bay was, that their land would not produce wheat, whereas, at the first settling of it, it is said that grain grew well, and came to a good degree of perfection; but we observed that they had almost wholly given over endeavouring to cultivate it, having been so often disappointed of having any increase, owing to a kind of blast that commonly took it after it had shot up into ear. Their chief grain is rye and indian corn, tho' but poor, of which they make their bread mostly.

6th Day, 29*th*.—We have been two months from home to-day. Very early our dear Friends Mary Ridgway, Jane Watson, Samuel Rodman and wife, &c., parted with us, in order to pursue their journey further eastward; and we, after staying the morning at Salem, and dining at Captain Needham's, and having a parting sitting at James Needham's, set forward with Eunice Fitch, and reached her habitation at Medford, 15 miles, in the evening. Here we took up our quarters for the night.

This Friend has, within these few years, been convinced of our principles, and after enduring many deep trials and exercises, on various accounts, is now become a grave, solid woman, and accepted as a member among us, and my desire on her account is, that she may be preserved to hold her integrity to the end—that so she may finish her course in peace with the Lord, which is the crown of all our labours in this world.

7th Day, 30*th*.—Rode 5 miles to Boston, and there spent the day, going round to see several Friends.—This town, about which I walked several times, is an irregularly built place; the streets narrow, and paved with pebble stone, without a brick foot-way, which renders it unpleasant and painful to the feet. The buildings are mostly of wood, but many of the houses large and roomy, neatly painted and ornamented.

The police is well attended to, and on First-day remarkably quiet and orderly. The Presbyterian Meeting Houses are spacious buildings, and the people zealous in frequenting their places of worship;—very civil in their deportment towards strangers, and much moderated in their sentiments towards those who differ from them in religious sentiments.

1*st Day*, 31*st*.—At a small Meeting in the forenoon, my companion had a few words to communicate; in the afternoon he was larger in testimony. He had been under much exercise of mind in Boston, and thought he should not be clear without appointing a Meeting for the inhabitants generally. Upon application to the Select-men, as they are called, they readily granted the use of Faneuil Hall, and the 4th hour to-morrow was fixed on for the time of gathering. In the evening Thomas had some satisfactory service in a family sitting at our lodgings.

2*d Day*, 1*st of Eighth month*.—My beloved companion, having for the greater part of the time since our coming to Boston, been greatly distressed and exercised in his mind, and seeing no way to get relief but by appointing a public Meeting, it was, agreeable to appointment, held to-day at Faneuil Hall, where a large number of people of different denominations assembled. He was enabled to ease his mind of a heavy burden, and I hope no injury was done to the cause of Truth, but that the opportunity might prove useful to some.

3d Day, 2*d*.—Last evening and this morning visited most if not all the families of Friends in this town—about 6 in number. After dinner at Griffith Barney's, set out for Lynn, where we arrived about 4, at the house of our kind friend Samuel Collins, who had set out from Boston to conduct us to his house, but we missed seeing him.

In the afternoon we took a pleasant walk, about half a mile, to the sea-shore, where we had a full view out to sea. This is a rocky, iron-bound shore for many miles along the coast.

4th Day, 3*d*.—At the Week-day Meeting at Lynn, made up mostly of Friends, Cousin Thomas was fervently engaged to discharge his duty on behalf of the great cause which had drawn him from his family and near connections in life, and ability was afforded to impart his prospects and feelings in a manner that took sensible hold of the minds of most that were present, so that I hope the audience received benefit and encouragement through his labour of love.

This town of Lynn is the place which some Friends have in view to remove the Yearly Meeting to; and I think it is not improbable that it may take place at some future time. After the conclusion of the Meeting for Worship, the Preparative Meeting was held; after which we dined and went forward to Salem, and lodged at James Needham's.

5th Day, *4th*.—At Meeting at Salem to-day; my companion was favoured with an open good time—the most so, I think, of any since we have been out together. He was also concerned to communicate something in love and tenderness at Jas. Needham's, before we parted, which was, with many tears, about 4.

After we got to our lodgings at Boston, most of the Friends of note of that place being present, he had, for the last time, an opportunity to relieve his mind, and was plain and honest in his labour, which I earnestly desire may tend to strengthen that which remains in some minds, which may be ready to die.

6th Day, *5th*.—Was up this morning at day-break, and on the road about half after four. Taking our leave of Boston, we breakfasted, about 9 miles on our way to Providence, at Dedham, the place where they formerly banished our dear Friends to, then a wilderness; at least they sent them so far on their way into the desert, and so left them to take their chance among the wild beasts and Indians, who were, in some instances, kinder than their bloody-minded persecutors.

Baited at the "Buck," and dined at the "Crown," and so went on, and baited once more before we reached Moses Brown's, at Providence, which, I think, we made a 50-mile ride to-day, by reason of missing our way. So it was about dark when we got into our quarters, and we were a good deal fagged and weary.

The road from Boston to Providence is not a bad one for this country, take it all together, and being a Post road, is attended to a little more than the cross-country roads, which are abounding in stones. These stones might be reckoned a part of the riches of this country, if they would build good houses of them, but they seem prejudiced against them, as we don't see one stone house among five hundred, according to my observation.

7th Day, 6*th.*—Had a good night's rest, after yesterday's hard ride, and spent the morning agreeably in Moses Brown's family, who was kind and respectful. After dinner, he invited us to go to Providence, about a mile from his house. Here we had a view of the cotton manufactory of velvets, corduroys, and jeans, which appeared in a prosperous way.

Met our friend and townsman, James Bringhurst, and had some account by him from home. Drank tea at Wm. Almy's, Moses Brown's son-in-law, after which we went home with Moses, and had a good night's rest under his roof.

1*st Day*, 7*th.*—The morning Meeting at Providence was held in silence, about 60 or 70 persons present. In the afternoon, my companion had something to communicate, which, I believe, was well received. Visited Job Scott's family, he having lately buried his wife, who has left a number of children behind. He appeared supported under his affliction, and much resigned under so trying a dispensation.

At Thomas Arnold's we had a short sitting. Cousin Thomas was concerned to mention the danger of looking back to Egypt, after having in a measure experienced a deliverance from the bondage and captivity of Pharoah and his hard task-masters; and also some further knowledge of the work of true religion. We then returned to our lodgings at Moses Brown's, he and his kind and affectionate wife being with us. Moses observed that Thomas was here favoured to hit the mark in his religious communication.

2d Day, 8th.—This morning was chiefly spent in free and friendly converse. About noon came up a fine rain, which was truly acceptable to the thirsty land, which stood much in need of it—having been near three months much parched with drouth hereaway.

After it cleared away, we went with our friend Brown and his wife to visit some Friends in the town of Providence, where my companion had some suitable matter to deliver in several family sittings, and came home to our lodgings in peace.

I had to-day an opportunity of going through Providence, which I don't think very pleasantly situated, lying under, or rather on the side of, a great hill. It contains two principal streets, about a mile and a half long.

The buildings are mostly wood; some are of brick, but few of them elegant. The Baptist Meeting House, however, must be allowed to have a spacious appearance, with a costly steeple, which, I think, exceeds either of ours in Philadelphia.

There are several persons who carry on trade in a shipping way to a considerable extent. I was shown the place where a large ship of 900 tons was lately built, which is now on her voyage to India. The land around this place is light and sandy, much like the Jerseys.

3d Day, 9th.—This was a fine rainy day, which was a pleasing sight to many who depend upon the culture of the ground for bread. Divers Friends stopped and lodged at this house on their way to Portsmouth Quarterly Meeting. Employed myself in writing several pieces I thought worth preserving.

In the evening we had a sitting in the family, in which my beloved companion was largely engaged to extend council and warning to several states present, particularly the younger part of the household, which I wish may be remembered at a future day, and the snares of the Enemy of all Righteousness avoided by the simple and unwary, whom he is watching to betray and deceive.

4th Day, 10th.—Rose early, and set out with Moses Brown and several other Friends. We crossed a small ferry near Providence, and another at a little town called Warren. Afterwards we came to Bristol Ferry, where we once more came in sight of the Garden of America—Rhode Island.

We got well over about 10 o'clock, and called at Benjamin Freeborn's, where we partook of some refreshment. Then went to Jacob Mott's, with an intention to stay 'till the Quarterly Meeting to-morrow.

5th Day, 11th.—The Quarterly Meeting was held at Portsmouth, at the north end of Rhode Island. It was a large Meeting, consisting of 7 Monthly Meetings, and it is remarkable that tho' Friends are so numerous hereaways, there are but very few Ministering Friends; our friend Job Scott is one of the most noted belonging to this quarter, and Patience Brayton another—she belongs to Swansey. Job and Cousin Thomas were both engaged for the good of the people. May a blessing attend their honest labour.

The business was finished about 5, and we rode through the rain to our quarters, where we partook of a late dinner with many other Friends from divers parts.

The rain continued all night, 'Tis likely this may produce a fresh vegetation, which hath been much stagnated by several months' dry weather. A good bed, after such an exercising day, was very comfortable and refreshing;—moreover, here our poor horse fared well.

6th Day, 12*th*.—This day it cleared away, and many Friends came to our quarters, it being a house much noted for the entertainment of Friends. My companion had a good time in a family sitting. Afterwards I had a good time to write to my dear wife. Cousin Thomas also wrote to his family.

In the afternoon we went off the island, to the Widow Barker's, at Tiverton, crossing a ferry about as wide as our Schuylkill. This was a very pleasant ride; we met with good accommodations, and kind entertainment. James Bringhurst and wife were with us, and very friendly.

7th Day, 13*th*.—Dear Thomas, finding his mind opened so far as to appoint a Meeting, notice was accordingly given, and a considerable number of Friends and others assembled about the 11th hour.

He was quickly ready to communicate what he was furnished with in exhortation and encouragement respecting the greatest of all concernments, to wit: the everlasting welfare of the immortal soul—which, 'tis hoped, had a tendency to strengthen and invigorate *that* in some which had long languished, and even been nearly extinguished.

They had been so remiss and lukewarm in the attendance of their Week-day Meeting, that the Monthly Meeting of Salem, to which they belonged, apprehended it most proper to put down their Weekday Meeting, as there did not appear a disposition to keep it up with that zeal and reputation which is proper and necessary to protect it from reproach.

He had also a good service in a sitting with the family after we had dined. About 4 we recrossed the ferry, and came to Newport in the dusk of the evening.

I retired to bed early, having been much afflicted the latter part of the day with a bad fit of the sick headache, as severe as any I have had since I left my own home. My kind friends at our lodging manifested much tenderness and affection towards me. In the morning it went off, and I was enabled to go on as usual with what my hands found to do in necessary concerns, writing to my dear partner, &c., and truly, I did not lack employment of one kind or other.

1*st Day*, 14*th*.—At forenoon and afternoon Meetings my companion was exercised in his gift in the Ministry with good authority. His labour of love appeared to have good place in the minds of the people, who behaved with becoming solidity and quietude. This being the last Meeting we were like to have at Newport, the opportunity was favourable for him to clear himself, so as to depart in peace.

Dined at our friend John Hadwen's, and drank tea at Giles Hosier's, where Cousin Thomas was again commissioned to dispense a portion of the Word to divers states present who were labouring under discouragements. He was also concerned to speak again in the evening at Thomas Robinson's, remarkably to some of the younger branches of the family. So this day was spent, I hope, not without some degree of profit, both to ourselves and others.

2d Day, 15*th*.—Dispatched a long letter to my dear wife, and just after I had sealed it, our townsman John Warder brought me three from my dear family.

These letters contained an account of the decease of my wife's father, John Elliott, in great peace, as his life had been circumspect and virtuous. We are favoured with a comfortable hope that he is released in mercy from the troubles and afflictions of time, and admitted into those mansions of happiness prepared for the righteous.

He was about 78 years of age, and had for some considerable time been in a great measure helpless, by reason of a paralytic disorder, which in a great measure deprived him of the use of his limbs. It also affected his speech.

He died the first of the present month, about 3 o'clock in the morning, and left a good savour behind him, both among Friends and others.

We dined to-day at Thomas Robinson's, with a number of other Friends. Afterwards paid several short visits at Mary Rodman's, Elizabeth Huntington's, and Ann Carpenter's, at all which places Cousin Thomas was concerned in testimony.

His gift in families, as well as more publicly, is large, clear, and instructive, and his labour from family to family, where our lot hath been cast, has been well received, and generally had a considerable reach on the minds of those present, so that they were often broken into tenderness, and I hope the seed thus sown may produce an increase to the praise and honour of the Great and Good Husbandman, and also to the furtherance and building up of the sincere in heart in the Way of Life and Salvation.

3d Day, 16*th*.—Dined this day at our lodgings, and after dinner went about 7 miles to Isaac Lawton's. Soon after we got there, we walked over to Job Almy's, and had a sitting in his family, in which my companion expressed what weighed upon his spirit. We then took our leave, and returned to Isaac Lawton's. About bed-time, had a gust of rain, with thunder and lightning.

4th Day, 17*th*.—This was their Week-day Meeting in course at Portsmouth, which we attended. My companion had a good service, and was favoured to leave them in a good degree of clearness.

Dined at Jacob Mott's; afterwards had a sitting in his family, in which Cousin Thomas was concerned to press the necessity of a devotedness of heart to follow the Divine requirings, as the only condition of being in a state of acceptance, when the solemn summons shall call us out of time into that state of everlasting fixedness, towards which we are with swift advances hastening.

In the afternoon called to see our antient Friend James Mitchel, and came to Newport seasonably in the evening. In a family sitting at our lodgings, my companion was large and fervent in his labour for the good of those present, who were much affected.

5th Day, 18*th, and* 6*th Day*, 19*th.*—This day we concluded to embark with Capt. Lawton for New York. We spent the morning in taking leave of our kind friends, and getting our horse and chaise on board. Afternoon, had a sitting in the family of our kind landlord, John Hadwen, in which my companion was engaged to commemorate the Lord's goodness in carrying through His dependent children to the praise of His Name; and a word of encouragement to trust and confide in His Fatherly Protection and Providence —about 25 being present.

We then walked down to the vessel, accompanied by a number of friends, and set sail from Newport about the 10th hour, with a fair wind. At 11 we passed the Light House on the point of Connanicut Island, and opened the main ocean, the wind about north, and a pleasant easy gale.

Did not feel disposed to be sick, but rather an appetite to food. About noon, the wind came more to the east, and fair. We went before it at about 5 or 6 knots an hour.

Passing Block Island, we had sight of Montauk Point, on Long Island, about 2, and still going on with a fair small breeze, we passed New London Light House, and so into what is properly called the Sound, where the navigation is reckoned more safe.

Our Captain, as usual, put on his watch-coat and stood the deck all night, which made us easy to go into our berths, and compose ourselves to rest for the night.

Our fellow-passengers were one man, three women, two servants and one child, for all of whom we had good accommodations, and so were very comfortable. Our horse, in the hold, seemed as well content as if he were in a stable, and eat his hay and oats with an appetite.

Between 12 and 1, I turned out of my berth and went upon deck, and found we were under fine way, about eight knots an hour. The wind being steady, the Peggy had but little motion, so we were free from sickness—the bilge-water being at rest, which commonly turns the stomachs of the passengers not used to travelling by water.

We had, however, *one* inconvenience to encounter—that was, *a great number* of fleas, which were busily employed in getting their livings out of us.

About 1 o'clock it began to rain, and the vessel to have a considerable motion. However, as we still made good way towards our desired port, it kept up our spirits, and we had an appetite for a bit of good cheese and porter, of which we had some of the best on board.

When the day dawned, we had run nearly two-thirds of our passage. The rain and wind increased, yet we were not uncomfortable in the cabin.

About 12 at noon we went through the narrow passage, by some called Hell Gate, (but I think a better name would be Whirl Gate). About half after two we landed at New York, having had a good passage of 28 hours.

May our minds be properly impressed with a sense of the protection and providence of the Great Preserver. Lodged at James Parson's, where we were kindly accommodated.

7th Day, 20*th*.—Wrote a letter to my friends at Newport, and part of one to my dear wife. Afterwards went down to Capt. Lawton's vessel, and had my horse and chaise landed. Then took a ride with James Parsons, Jun., to stretch my horse's legs, after standing in the hold, and found him in good spirits. Had some of the harness repaired.

Dined at Henry Haydock's; he had five daughters at the table. Afternoon, went to see our townsfolks, Jonathan Shoemaker and wife and company, at their lodgings at John Murry's. Then called to see Nathaniel Clark and John Dean's families, and so home and to rest.

1*st Day*, 21*st*.—At Meeting in the forenoon— which was silent. Dined at Benjamin Haviland's, who kindly offered to accompany us to Rahway.— About 3 we went on board the boat, and landed at Elizabethtown Point in about two hours and a quarter, the distance is called 15 miles.

Got to Joseph Shotwell's, at Rahway, before 7, when divers of our old friends came in to see us—my companion being particularly beloved in this place.

2*d Day*, 22*d*.—This was the Quarterly Meeting at Rahway, and the gathering large, many people of other Societies being there, some of them very light and airy in their spirits.

My companion sat a considerable time in silence, yet at length was favoured in a full, clear, and well-accepted testimony, before the Meeting separated, and also at the conclusion, when the partition between the men and women was opened, in order that what he had to say might be heard on both sides of the house.

Dined at John Haydock's. Afterwards called in to see Isaac Martin, Henry Shotwell, and John Shotwell. Then went home, and had a sitting at our lodging, where Cousin Thomas was again concerned to speak to the edification and comfort of those present, several of whom were much tendered. Wrote to my dear wife,—and so this day finished.

3d Day, 23*d*.—The Youth's Meeting was this day held, which may be called a high day, if not an holy day—my companion being enabled to preach the Gospel in a degree of the Power and authority which ever accompanies a true and living Ministry—proceeding from the Divine Fountain of Love, after which he concluded the Meeting in prayer.

Dined with many Friends at Joseph Shotwell's. Drank tea at Isaac Martin's. Afterwards had a satisfactory sitting at our lodgings, with about 20 Friends, and then retired to rest.

4th Day, 24*th*.—Arose before day, and got on the road a little before 5, and enjoyed the refreshing exhalations of a Summer's morning, which was exceedingly reviving to nature.

Took a second breakfast at Brunswick, and proceeded for Princeton. Reached Robert White's about 1 o'clock, which is called 34 miles. Here my companion felt easy to make a halt and rest ourselves, the day being very warm. So we got our dinner, and spent the afternoon agreeably at our kind friend's house, where our horse and ourselves were well provided for.

My beloved companion, in this day's ride, expressed more fully than usual his satisfaction and peace of mind, in being thus favoured to accomplish our journey so far, and signified that he thought himself clear of New England.

He had been at times much exercised, both in mind and body, and I had an opportunity of being a witness of the arduous engagement that such an undertaking necessarily creates.

Indeed, were it not for Divine assistance, it could not be performed, and gone through, with real profit, either to the individual or the people—but, through Holy Help, the poor baptized instrument is supported from day to day; and strength and ability mercifully vouchsafed by the Great Master to His humble, dependent children.

5th Day, 25*th*.—Was out of bed about 4; a thick, foggy morning, which presaged a warm day, and so it proved. I thought it the warmest I had felt since I left home.

Reached Isaac Collins' at Trenton, about 7, and took a second breakfast. Went up into his printing room, where his hands were busily employed on a quarto edition of the Holy Bible, which they were near finishing;—a great work, and, I believe, the first of the size printed in America.

He told us he meant to strike off 5,000 impressions, which would occasion him to advance, in paper and workmanship, at least from £4,000 to £5,000, before he could receive any advantage. But, as our Society in the United States, and particularly in Pennsylvania, have encouraged the work, by subscription and otherwise, I hope his laudable and industrious endeavours may be finally blessed and prospered.

Put on from Trenton; crossed the Delaware, and got to Samuel Moon's, by the Falls Meeting House, half an hour before Meeting time.

This Quarterly Meeting for Bucks County is very large. Several Friends appeared in short testimonies—my companion was one.

Meeting held 'till 3, and after we got into our quarters, there came on the heaviest rain that I had seen for many months, attended with thunder and lightning; and so we were weather-bound, and prevented from going to a Friend's house, a few miles distant.

However, towards evening it abated, and we went to Jonathan Kirkbride's as the night shut in. A number of other Friends also lodged at this house, being large, and a place long noted for entertaining Friends.

6th Day, 26*th*.—This also proved a very hot day. For that reason set off early for Meeting, that we might have a little time to rest at a Friend's house before we went in.

Our horse, also, after such a long journey, was somewhat worn down, tho' his spirits did not fail, and he performed well on the whole.

At Meeting, Samuel Wilson appeared first, then Cousin Thomas was large and fervent, spending and being spent for the good of the people—and truly, if such favours are not prized, and the visitations of Divine kindness and love joined in with, I fear it may prove as an hand-writing against us in the awful Day of Account.

Dined at Samuel Moon's, and afterwards set off for Bristol, and lodged at Phineas Buckley's.

7th Day, 27*th*.—Wrote a letter to my dear wife early this morning, and sent it by a person going directly to Philadelphia. Afterwards crossed over to Burlington.

Here we met with many Friends who came from the neighbouring parts to attend the Quarterly Meeting, to be held here on Second-day.

We dined at Elizabeth Barker's, and drank tea and lodged at John Hoskins'.

1st Day, 28*th*.—At morning Meeting at Burlington, my companion first had a favoured time; then our friend Solomon Gaskill, and then Cousin Thomas concluded the Meeting in prayer. Dined at John Cox's.

About 3 my two sons, John and Caleb, came up in the stage-boat from Philadelphia, which afforded me much satisfaction and pleasure, in seeing them, and hearing more particularly from my dear wife and friends at home.

Afternoon Meeting was silent. Tea at Daniel Smith's, and having spent the evening agreeably, we went to rest in good season.

2d Day, 29*th*.—This proved the hottest day, according to my apprehension, of any I have experienced or felt this Summer.

The Quarterly Meeting for business began, as usual, at the 11th hour. Huson Longstreth appeared in public testimony with good acceptance. There being much business, the sitting was long, and trying to weak constitutions. The Meeting concluded about 5. Dined at John Hoskins', with many other Friends, and was pretty well carried through this very warm day.

3d Day, *30th*.—After a sultry night, were glad to get into the fresh morning air, and so rose early. Was favoured to be pretty clear of my head-ache. About 10, the heat increased nearly equal to what it was yesterday.

The Youth's Meeting was much thronged; neverthless, the fervent labourers in the vineyard were enabled to lift up their voices—Rebecca Brown first, then Mary Newbold; after her Benjamin Clark, and then my companion, all in a good degree of clearness and Gospel authority, so that light and chaffy spirits were, as it were, commanded into silent attention, and the Meeting was covered with solid weight.

Our Friend Rebecca Wright closed the service in supplication, in which the hearts of many present feelingly joined in ascribing praise where only it is due.

After dining, we crossed Delaware River, and immediately set off in our chaise for Philadelphia, where we arrived about 8, and found our families well, and met with an affectionate reception.

Thus, having been enabled to perform this little Labour of Love in accompanying my beloved friend and cousin in this journey to some parts of New England, and having evidently experienced the Good Hand to be near to open the way for us, and strengthen us, in the work of His requiring, I was made truly thankful, and now desire to render the praise and honour to Him who is alone worthy—forever more.

THE END
OF MY
NEW ENGLAND JOURNEY.

I NOW GO ON WITH

Short Notes on the Time

AS IT PASSED AT HOME.

4th Day, 8th Mo. 31st, 1791.

I had a severe fit of the head-ache to-day, and kept in-doors on that account. Several friends kindly called to see us.

5th Day, 1*st of Ninth month.*—The rain yesterday evening laid the dust, and made the air cooler. Was employed in some necessary matters, which required my attention.

6th Day, 2*d.*—In looking after my outward concerns, found my mind calmed and comforted, in a sense of the goodness and mercy of the Great Preserver and Upholder of all His dependent children, who rely upon Him, and have no other confidence— and at the same time are not slothful in doing what their hands find to do, both inwardly and outwardly; for we cannot expect the blessing to be added unless we do our part.

7th Day, 3*d.*—A wet day, which kept me mostly within doors, where I was employed in writing and attending to some friends who kindly called.

1st Day, 4*th*.—Attended three Meetings to-day, to my comfort. The weather continues dull.

2d Day, 5*th*.—Much rain to-day and last night, which confined me to the house mostly.

3d Day, 6*th*.—Attended Week-day Meeting, and had an opportunity of speaking to many friends, who kindly welcomed me home.

4th Day, 7*th*.—Went out to see several friends at their own houses; and when at home proceeded in transcribing the notes I had made of my New England Journey. Mother Elliott came up to stay a day or two with us.

5th Day, 8*th*.—Cleared up fine, but warm. Was at High Street Meeting, where I heard divers weighty communications.

6th Day, 9*th*.—A dull day, tho' without much rain. In the afternoon, with my dear wife, took a ride a few miles, and found it pleasant, as there was no dust. Called at Samuel Fisher's place on Schuylkill, and drank tea with his sister Hetty. Then returned home about dark.

7th Day, 10*th*.—Was at home most of the day, and not uselessly employed.

1st Day, 11*th*.—At Meeting thrice. My dear Bell not very well. Mother Elliott poorly; went in the evening to see her.

2d Day, 12*th*.—Was engaged in writing to Nantucket. Afternoon, attended Overseer's Meeting.

3d Day, 13*th*.—At Week-day Meeting, Joseph James and Mary Hopkins, (daughter of Samuel,) were married. John Pemberton appeared in testimony, after which the Preparative Meeting was held.

4th Day, 14th.—This day was mostly spent in writing letters to some of my friends in New England.

5th Day, 15th.—Employed in doing a little carpenter's work, which I find useful as an exercise—conducing to circulate the blood, and keep the bodily machine in health.

6th Day, 16th.—Did something in the painting way, which I have been a little used to for many years.

7th Day, 17th.—Busy at home, most of the day, about my family concerns.

1st Day, 18th.—At morning Meeting Peter Yarnall had large and acceptable service, being favoured with a Gift equal to most in our Society, altho' in the earlier part of his life his conduct was wide from the Principle; but through Divine condescension and mercy, I trust, his present and future devotedness will be accepted as an atonement, and that he may continue a bright ornament to our Christian profession.

2d Day, 19th—Found employment at home agreeably—as I seldom want for something to be busy in, either pleasant or profitable; which I consider a favour, as it tends to make home comfortable, and, with a contented and resigned mind, to be my happiest place.

3d Day, 20th.—Monthly Meeting, which concluded about 2, there not being so much business as common.

4th Day, 21st.—Captain Needham arrived, and brought me an account from Friends to the Eastward; also, certificates for T. Scattergood and myself.

5th Day, 22d.—Rode a few miles with my wife, for the benefit of air and exercise. In the evening some rain fell.

6th Day, 23*d*.—A warm day for the season. Was taken up about trifles, which, perhaps, may be said to be the general employment of mankind, as everything which has not an ultimate tendency to make provision for the immortal part, may be considered as such; however, as we have bodies as well as souls, I believe it is allowable to make comfortable provision for them, as a secondary concern.

7th Day, 24*th*.—Friends began to collect, in order to attend the Yearly Meeting. Several from New York took up their quarters with us.

1st Day, 25*th*.—At morning Meeting our friend Robert Nesbit, from New England, exercised his gift in the Ministry, and had good service. Afternoon and evening were also comfortable Meetings.

2d Day, 26*th*.—The business of the Yearly Meeting opened at 10, and was resumed at 3. Considerable progress was made at these two sittings, having our friend Nicholas Waln for clerk, who is an able hand.

3d Day, 27*th*.—The business further proceeded on. Had the company of pretty many of our country Friends at our house.

4th Day, 28*th*.—*5th Day*, 29*th*.—*6th Day*, 30*th*.— These three days were much taken up on some services of the Meeting, and attending on Friends at our house.

7th Day, 1*st of Tenth month*.—This day the Yearly Meeting concluded, to general satisfaction, and many Friends went out of town.

1st Day, 2*d*.—Had a heavy fit of the head-ache, which confined me to the house through the day, not getting to either of the sittings for worship.

2d Day, 3*d.*—The New York Friends our lodgers, Benjamin Haviland, his daughter Mary, and Polly Titus, set off in the stage for that place.—Bought wood for our winter firing. Several friends to see us in the afternoon.

3d Day, 4*th.*—At Meeting Robert Nesbit appeared to satisfaction; also some others. My son Johnny set off for a little journey into the country, for his health, which latterly has not been so well as we could wish.

4th Day, 5*th.*—Finished getting my winter's wood in to-day. Walked so as to tire myself, but feeling my mind peaceful, it was enough.

5th Day, 6*th.*—At High Street Meeting, Robert Nesbit preached a close searching sermon on the love of money, and the over-anxious pursuit of worldly things. Had several Friends to dine with us to-day. The circumstances of life, how changeable and uncertain; and a good state, or a favoured state, how easily lost, and how hard to be regained.

6th Day, 7*th.*—Wrote several letters to friends at Newport, and rode out with my wife in the afte noon.

7th Day, 8*th.*—Was mostly engaged at home. Samuel Howell, brushmaker, deceased.

1st Day, 9*th.*—Attended three Meetings to-day, to my satisfaction.

2d Day, 10*th.*—Was at an appointed Meeting for the Young People of the City, held at the North Meeting House, at the request of Robert Nesbit, from Husack, in New England, who had a full opportunity for the relief of his exercised mind, in well-meant, honest labour for their profit. Nicholas Waln and William Savery also had good service.

3d Day, 11*th*.—Attended our Week-day Meeting in course, which was small in number, but comfortable.

4th Day, 12*th*.—Was busy at home in the morning. Afternoon visited a friend, with my wife.

5th Day, 13*th*.—Sister Gray set off on a visit to Maryland, in company with Isaac Howell and wife, and Isaac Elliott. Afternoon, visited a friend. Evening to see Mary Smith, who daily expects her husband.

6th Day, 14*th*.—Busied about secular concerns, which if kept within due bounds, (being necessary,) are not hurtful; they are only so in the excess. In the afternoon, arrived in town our beloved Friend Samuel Smith, from his religious visit to England and Ireland, to the joy of his wife and friends. George Dillwyn, also, with his wife, came in the same vessel. Received several letters from friends to the Eastward.

7th Day, 15*th*.—At a Special Meeting of the Ministers, Elders, and Overseers of the 3 Monthly Meetings in this city, by request of our Friend Robert Nesbit, who appeared clothed with much love in what he had to communicate. An exercise was manifested generally for the promotion of spiritual health of the Society, and for the putting away of such things as retard us in our progress towards the Heavenly rest.

1st Day, 16*th*.—At Meeting thrice, and I hope, received some benefit. S. Smith, G. Dillwyn, and

Robert Nesbit, all appeared in a degree of Gospel Authority.

2d Day, 17*th*.—At another Meeting of Ministers, Elders and Overseers, where much Christian freedom was exercised for our improvement in a spiritual relation.

3d Day, 18*th*.—Robert Nesbit left our city early this morning, by whom I wrote to a friend Eastward. Had a sitting at his lodgings at Catharine Greenleaf's, which I hope was profitable to some.

4th Day, 19*th*.—Got in two cords of stove wood, in addition to my winter store, so that I hope we may now look Winter in the face 'till the 4th Month at least, when Sol will be far advanced in his return to our Northern Hemisphere, and consequently, the face of nature revived and invigorated by his animating rays.

5th Day, 20*th*.—Johnny returned from a two weeks excursion into the country, for the benefit of air and exercise, which is so justly accounted conducive to health, and I think he has made out pretty well on the whole, considering he is but a young traveller.

6th Day, 21*st*.—Had some troublesome work on hand, with a bad tenant, who evidently designed to impose upon me as long as he could, and tho' I did not get all my due, yet I found means to get him out of my house.

7th Day, 22*d*.—Wrote a letter to a friend at Nantucket, and filled up the remainder of the day with other employment.

1st Day, 23*d*.—Attended three Meetings, at which was some edifying public service. How great are our opportunities for religious improvement in this city; perhaps beyond any other place.

2d Day, 24*th*.—Walked to Schuylkill, about some stone for a building I have in hand, which, however, wearied me a good deal; but I slept well the night following.

3d Day, 25*th*.—Monthly Meeting day—which held late, and was somewhat trying to some of us that had weak frames.

4th Day, 26*th*.—Was engaged in some troublesome necessary business of a temporal nature, in which however, I preserved my own peace, tho' I had to deal with a spiteful and malicious spirit, who had the will but not the power to do me an injury, except in my outward interest, which I did not much regard. This relates to a tenant of the name of Boggs.

5th Day, 27*th*.—Intended for Meeting, but an unexpected occurrence prevented.

6th Day, 28*th*.—Attended a committee on some Society business.

7th Day, 29*th*.—Was engaged in some temporal concerns. The weather, for a considerable time past, has been dry and dusty, so that the farmer thinks the winter-grain suffers; but we are a murmuring generation, and seldom satisfied with the dispensations meted out to us, which, nevertheless, are doubtless in unerring wisdom.

1*st Day*, 30*th*.—Attended three Meetings to-day, to good satisfaction.

2*d Day*, 31*st*.—Was busy about some repairs at my dwelling and the tenement adjoining.

3d Day, 1*st of Eleventh month.*—Attended our Week-day Meeting, and the adjournment of our Monthly Meeting afterwards. Afternoon, visited a friend, with my wife.

4th Day, 2*d.*—Spent the forenoon chiefly in writing. Afternoon, visited a friend. Evening, attended a committee on Meeting business. The town has, for some months, at times, been alarmed by fires—chiefly stables, and there is reason to believe they have been purposely fired by evil disposed persons. Much industry has been used to discover them, but as yet without effect. Patrols have been kept up about the streets at night, and $1,000 offered for apprehending the guilty offenders.

5th Day, 3*d.*—At Week-day Meeting, Jacob Lindley had the principal service by way of Ministry. The weather altered to-day from dry and dusty to wet, with a considerable fall of snow for the season.

6th Day, 4*th.*—A fair morning. Settled accounts with brother Joshua respecting my dear Aunt Mary Armitt's affairs. Had some other engagements on hand, which kept me much within-doors to-day.

7th Day, 5*th.*—Sundry Friends from the country came in to attend the Quarterly Meeting. Moderate pleasant weather.

1st Day, 6*th.*—At three Meetings as usual, which were favoured. My sight has been but poor, and I have been obliged to wear spectacles about four years.

2d Day, 7*th.*—The day of our Quarterly Meeting; the business finished at two sittings. The adjournment made so as to hold our next Quarterly

Meeting at the new or North Meeting House—the Fourth Street House, where it hath long been holden, being found, for some years, to be too small and inconvenient.

3d Day, 8*th*.—Youth's Meeting, at which H. Longstreth and William Savery exercised their Ministerial Gifts, I trust, to some good purpose; and, altho' some of the honest, fervent labourers are ready at times to conclude that there is little fruit produced by their repeated exercises, yet I think we may safely believe their religious labours have a secret tendency to keep us in the Holy Way, and encourage those who have not yet travelled in it to turn their feet thereinto; and also tend to discourage such as are habitually vicious from going the lengths which the Enemy of Souls would prompt them to. So that, on the whole, I believe a living Ministry to be a great blessing to the Church and to the community at large, and were it not for it, the land would become even more vile.

4th Day, 9*th*.—Employed mostly about home, and on some Meeting business. This I account my birth-day, and I now reckon I am entering my fiftieth year. O, that I may improve it to the best of purposes; that I may not be behind-hand when I am called to the awful bar, where every action, word and thought is to be judged, by Him to whom they are naked and open.

5th Day, 10*th*.—Was engaged in rendering some service to a young person who, by his misconduct, has brought himself into much exercise and trouble, so that I did not go to Meeting to-day. Happy for them who look to the inward Instructor, the safe and sure Guide thro' the wilderness of this world, and a favour it is, when we see that we have missed our way, to endeavour to get back again as fast as we can, and let the time past suffice in which we have been doing our own wills, and offering violence to that inspeaking Word and Voice, that will not only *show* us the right way, but give us *power* and ability to walk therein.

6th Day, 11*th*.—My dear wife, with several other Friends, by appointment of the Quarterly Meeting, attended Haverford Monthly Meeting. It being a fine, pleasant day, they returned in good season in the evening. The report was that the visit was acceptable to the visited, and satisfactory to the visitors. N. Waln and Hannah Cathrall were two of the number.

7th Day, 12*th*.—Was engaged about some writing relative to my dear Aunt's estate.

1*st Day*, 13*th*.—Attended 3 Meetings, as usual.

2*d Day*, 14*th*.—In the morning was employed at home, about outward concerns. Afternoon, attended a general Meeting of Ministers, Elders, and Overseers for the city. In the evening, was at a Meeting of the Overseers for our own particular Meeting.

3*d Day*, 15*th*.—At Week-day Meeting in course, after which the Preparative Meeting was held. Afternoon, mostly at home, Mother Elliott being at our house for a few days.

4*th Day*, 16*th*.—Agreed with Nathan A. Smith to build several tenements for me on Cresson's Alley, having a piece of ground there which I think may be best for me to improve.

5th Day, 17*th*.—At High Street Meeting House, Samuel Coates and Amy Horner married. Went to see a friend in the evening.

6th Day, 18*th*.—Filled up my time with writing, reading, and necessary care of my family and outward concerns, not forgetting, I hope, things of higher importance; but it's no small attainment to keep always right, or in other words, in the true resignation, and get the selfish part enough in subjection.

In the evening, went out to see a friend, for I find it is not best to live alone, and that much true comfort arises from affectionate intercourse, whether it be in the line of outward relationship, or out of that circle, so that it be on the bottom of true love, without sinister ends, and in that lovely sincerity which I have sometimes thought stamps or seals our actions either good or bad, as they do or do not arise from this noble spring or source.

7th Day, 19*th*.—Trimmed my vines, in order to lay them down, to protect them from the power of the winter's frost, which often checks them too much, tho' I find they will bear a moderate degree of cold without much injury.

Yet, as we are uncertain how the winter may prove, I choose to be, as the saying is, of the sure or safe side, especially as my vines are young, not many of them above two years old the coming spring; they bore some few bunches of fruit last season. Mother Elliott went home this evening.

1st Day, 20*th*.—Attended Meetings as usual, which, while I am favoured with tolerable health, I find to be an indispensable duty, from which many advantages constantly arise; for, attended in a right manner, and the mind as much as possible gathered to its proper center, it sweetens our spirits, and makes us more fit for the common duties of life; and together with corresponding conduct in our outward concerns amongst men, in our several capacities—social, moral, and religious—keeps us, in a good degree, in a state of preparation for our great and final change, which ought ever to be kept in view, as human life is confessedly altogether uncertain in every stage.

Indeed, when we consider our present state of being as a state of trial and warfare with our own hearts, lusts, and a host of external enemies upon every quarter, it is my solid judgment, (fixed from long experience,) that there is no true happiness independent of this state of holy preparation to meet our God; for the pleasures, profits, and honours of the world, most assuredly, will be proved to be insufficient to this great end.

Solomon himself confessed, when experience had made him wise, that they were indeed but vanity and vexation of spirit, and so I believe has every son of Adam found them in the closing awful scene which awaits us all.

My dear children, for whom I principally write, and for whom I am most affectionately concerned, as you, I trust, have in some good measure known the Truth, and been acquainted with its holy restraints, in the secret of your own breasts, my desire is that you may prize it above all earthly things. Let it appear to you as the pearl of great price hid in the field, (mark *hid*,) in the field of your hearts, for the purchase of which the rich merchantman sold or parted with his all.

And when you do so, you need never to fear but that all things necessary and really profitable will be added, and that neither grace nor glory, nor any good thing will be withheld.

O, that you may choose this richest of all blessings as your portion and the lot of your inheritance, and then I may humbly hope, that when mine and your precious mother's places on earth are known no more, that you will stand in our gap, and be as standard bearers amongst a dissipated generation.

For I have sometimes indulged a secret, humble hope, that of you it may be said, as of the untamed colt which our blessed Saviour sent his disciples for, formerly, and on which he made his triumphant entry into the Holy City, or that which was so called, (Jerusalem,) "*the Lord hath need of him*," or you.

For I believe, to each of you, his love and gracious compassion is eminently extended, and he would most assuredly gather you into his most blessed family. If you are but obedient to his Divine call, and devote the prime of your days to his ever-blessed service, he will take away your dross, and tin, and reprobate silver, and establish you as pillars in his house, (in due time,) and your ends will be crowned with peace and joy unutterable.

But if, unhappily, my dearest children, in your blooming years and spring-time of life, you turn aside from his holy commandment, and join yourselves to the people of the land, and buy and sell their merchandize, and traffic in their wares, or in other words, be united to their spirit and tempers, and follow their customs and maxims, then believe me, when I say you will most assuredly make to yourselves a long wilderness of affliction, which you may possibly be so entangled in as never to be able to get out of. And if you should fall there, as that murmuring people of old did, and never behold the good land, and blessed port and haven of rest, how would my poor head weep (if possible) for you in secret places, and all the powers of parental affection be on the utmost stretch for your deliverance and salvation from so deplorable a state.

But, my dearest children, I hope, and permit me to hope on a proper ground, better things of you; and such things as accompany salvation; and that He who, I most humbly hope, hath begun the good work, will, according to the good pleasure of His Divine and ever blessed will, carry it on, and in His own due and appointed time, perfect the same to His own Glory and your ever-enduring peace and happiness.

These few hints have arisen in my mind this evening, without the least premeditation, and wrote as fast as my hand could well go without any copy, and, as I know they are designed for your everlasting good, may you make the proper use of them, and then my end, and aim, and desire on your behalf, will be answered and completed.

During the Evening Meeting this day a fire broke out, and burnt down Cousin Jeremiah Cresson's stable, which unsettled the Meeting. Some kept their seats, but most of the assembly went out—a part of whom returned again before the Meeting concluded.

2d Day, 21*st*.—This morning I was taken with a great pain in the small of my back, as I was dressing, which occasioned me to keep my bed three days, part of which time I could scarcely move, tho' sundry applications and medicines were administered, and I was bled in my arm.

3*d Day*, 22*d*.—4*th Day*, 23*d*.—Was very much indisposed.

5*th Day*, 24*th*.—Was favoured to feel a little better, and made a shift to get out of bed and sit by the fire, but was much incommoded with pains, which I judged to be either the rheumatism or something of the gravel. I had no fever, nor a sick stomach, yet could scarcely rise out of a chair, or change my posture, without great uneasiness.

6*th Day*, 25*th*.—7*th Day*, 26*th*.—Perceived myself to mend slowly, so that with some difficulty I walked a little about my chamber, and had some appetite to eat, 'tho but sparingly.

1*st Day*, 27*th*.—Was so much better that I encouraged my dear wife to set off on a little journey to Robinson and Exeter Monthly Meetings, which a Committee of Men and Women Friends were, by our last Quarterly Meeting, appointed to visit. Came down stairs about noon, but felt myself very weak.

2*d Day*, 28*th*.—Came down about breakfast-time in the morning, and walked a little way in the middle part of the day, but I thought I took some cold, as it proved rainy towards evening, which will make it unpleasant for my wife and the other Friends.

3*d Day*, 29*th*.—Attended our Week-day Meeting, but was not well enough to stay the adjournment of the Monthly Meeting. My two sons assisted me in laying down our grape vines, in order to protect them from the frost in the extreme part of the approaching cold season, as they are mostly young, and not hardy enough to bear the severity of the winter.

4th Day, 30*th*.—A fine day for the season. I think 'tis likely my wife and company are at Maiden Creek Meeting to-day. Wrote several letters to some of my kind friends in New England, which I finished in the evening, in order to go by Captain Needham to Salem.

5th Day, 1*st of Twelfth month*.—This proved a stormy, wet day, which made me think a good deal of my wife and the other Women Friends on their journey in Berks County among the rugged hills, as she is of a delicate habit and frame, and not much abroad at this season of the year. Was very sick with the head-ache, the after part of the day.

6th Day, 2*d*.—A fine morning after the rain.— Captain Needham sailed to-day. I had an account of my wife's welfare a few days ago. Went to see a friend in the evening.

7th Day, 3*d*.—Another fine, healthy morning— tho' sharp, and hard-bound with the frost; the roads must be very rough. About noon my dear wife returned, having borne the fatigue of the journey quite well. In the evening, walked down to brother John's, to see our aged mother.

1st Day, 4*th*.—Sat three Meetings, which were highly favoured with instrumental labour. In the first, R. Jones and Samuel Emlen; afternoon, S. E., largely; evening, Peter Yarnall with great authority, and also in prayer.

2d Day, 5*th*.—A good deal of snow fell, but it did not lie long.

3d Day, 6*th*.—At Week-day Meeting, Griffith Edwards and Hannah Zane entered into marriage covenant. William Savery was concerned in testimony, with usual satisfaction to the auditory.

4th Day, 7*th*.—Was a cold winter-like day; some snow on the ground, though fine over-head. Was employed mostly in reading, and writing in my collection. How happy a contented mind, free from ambitious aims and worldly pursuits, satisfied with moderate things—fire, meat, and clothes—clothes, meat, and fire—as the poet says; and what need of more, or indeed, what *can* we enjoy more?

The abundance of wealth most certainly brings its cares and its perplexities; the pursuit of honour, fame, or worldly glory, abundant mortification and disappointment; pleasures are often attended with disgust, disease, and sometimes death and shame.

Let us, then, make our election and choice of those things which cloy not, neither perish with using; those durable riches that will not fail us beyond the narrow bounds of time, and that honour which cometh from God only.

And then we may, and often can, with entire freedom, leave the acquirement of earthly good to those who are so unwise as to barter that Heavenly birthright, to which they are entitled, if sought with proper earnestness, and suitable patience and perseverance.

However, I speak with caution, not as one that hath attained. I know the road to peace and happiness has its tribulations, baptisms and sufferings; nevertheless, as there is no other way to real glory but to endure and pass through them, let us cast our care upon Him who is alone able to succour His own humble dependent children, and then we may, with humble confidence, trust Him for the final event, and hope in His mercy that all things will end well.

5th Day, 8th.—At Week-day Meeting at High Street. Afternoon, attended the burial of Beulah Paschall, and then went with my Annabella to see a relation.

6th Day, 9th.—This day we hear of the dreadful overthrow of the Federal army, sent by Government into the Western Territory, with the avowed intention of destroying the poor Indians, and their towns, and winter's stock of provisions, which, to my apprehension, carries the appearance of tyranny, and an unjust invasion of native rights.

'Tis said 600 or 700 poor soldiers, many of them officers of distinction, were slain, and the remainder of the army, about 400 or 500, obliged to flee for their lives to the nearest fortification.

This being the second instance of a total defeat within two years, it greatly behooves our General Government to examine deeply whether their proceedings as to this deplorable Indian war are founded in justice and equity. And if they are not so founded, which it is much to be feared is really the case, how wise and honourable would it be to stay the sword, and desist from arbitrary force in compelling the native owners of the soil to abandon their claim to the country where the Beneficent Author and Creator of the universe hath placed and stationed them.

O, the unnumbered miseries that flow from the destructive principles of war to the human race. How much better would it have been, and how much more consistent with our religious profession as Christians, and our political claims as freemen making part of the great family of mankind, who are all equally entitled to their natural rights.

I say, how much better, and more to our honour, would it have been for us to have appropriated a small part of the treasure which has been so wantonly wasted in these last two campaigns into the Western country, for the promotion of peace with the natives, as a fourth part, (and perhaps a great deal less,) I believe, would have bought as much of their lands as the white people could have settled for these one hundred years to come, and also have promoted or established a peace with them which might have continued for a length of years.

7th Day, 10*th*.—Was not very well to-day.

1*st Day*, 11*th*.—Being somewhat better, attended two Meetings at the North Meeting House, and one in the evening at High Street. In the time of the sitting of the latter, an alarm of fire was given, but was soon over. However, it might have proved very serious had it not quickly been extinguished, as some great villain had set fire to a wisp of hay in a stable behind Hains' brew house, which, had it communicated to that in the loft above, might have made terrible destruction in that close-built part of the city.

2d Day, 12*th.*—Snow on the ground, and a cold winter day.

3d Day, 13*th.*—Attended Week-day Meeting in course. John Forster buried.

4th Day, 14*th.*—The air keen and sharp, yet wholesome and bracing to the body. I think much of the wretched remnant of the poor defeated army to the Westward. We learn, by late accounts from the General, Arthur St. Clair, that it is too true, that more than one-half of the whole army were cut off.

No doubt, among those whom they have reserved as captives, many will be put to most cruel torture, according to the savage Indian customs.

Many vigorous young men from the Eastern and Middle States have met an untimely end in the dreadful conflict, and no doubt parents, wives and children are in deep mourning for their unhappy fate.

5th Day, 15*th.*—At High Street Meeting, tho' I did not feel well. These frequent indispositions I consider as intimations from a Divine hand that the end of all things, as to this state of being here below, is drawing on, if not near. May I make a proper use of them, and be concerned more and more to set my house (or heart) in order for the awful time when a final separation must inevitably take place, and the dust return to its native dust.

O, then, to have a well-grounded, humble hope of acceptance and salvation in the realms of everlasting light and love. This, indeed, appears often to my view as the highest and most important of all concerns, compared with which the things of time and mortality are as trifling shadows, which appear and disappear, and are forever lost and gone. Mayest thou, then, O my soul, pursue the road to bliss and true happiness with increasing vigilance and firmness.

That as thy days shorten, and the shadows of evening are lengthening over thine head, thou mayest witness an increase in circumspection of life and conversation, a growth in true godliness, by and through the help and assistance of the Grace or Good Spirit, which as a Friend at hand, and a principle in which there is indeed power from God afforded to resist evil, and cleave to the good.

That, by the virtue of this Divine Principle, the great work may go on, and in due time be perfected, to the praise of the Divine and most Holy Name, and the everlasting well-being of the immortal spirit.—Amen.

6th Day, 16*th*.—Last night and to-day was greatly afflicted with my old complaint. Our European Friends, Mary Ridgway and Jane Watson, came to town in the evening.

7th Day, 17*th*.—Fatigued myself with some necessary employment. Find it best to be busy in moderation. The most satisfaction arises from engagements which are beneficial to ourselves or others, and tend to strengthen the good and discourage the evil propensity in us.

Man is formed for activity, and his senses and outward organs of the body adapted to various uses and ends in the creation. Let them, nevertheless, be employed in subservience to the all-important object, or at least innocently.

1st Day, 18*th*.—This was a very wet day, and walking excessively sloppy. However, attended three Meetings, as long has been my custom on this day of the week, when at home and well. They were comfortable, and I hope, in some degree, profitable. We have need *daily* of spiritual as well as outward food for our bodies' sustenance and health.

John Parrish, Thomas Scattergood, Sarah Harrison, and Mary Ridgway appeared. Peter Marriott and Mary Elmslie interred. A stable or store-house in Third Street burnt down. Supposed to have been set on fire by some wicked incendiaries, the like infamous practice having been continued for some months back.

2d Day, 19*th*.—This day a little boy who lived with Charles Wharton, 14 or 15 years old, was committed to prison, on suspicion of having been one at least, (if not a principal,) in setting fire to divers stables and out-buildings which have been burnt of late weeks. 'Tis said, indeed, that he has confessed the fact, which, if really true, is an instance how powerful the grand Seducer and Enemy of mankind is, even in early life, to draw the simple and unguarded into action and conduct destructive of every prospect of happiness, both outwardly and inwardly.

But such, alas, in too many instances, is the depravity of human nature, and what more can the virtuous mind do, in most instances, but lament without the power of redressing it.

Went with my wife in the evening to visit our European Friends, who make their homes at John Pemberton's.

3d Day, 20*th*.—Week-day Meeting, Jane Watson appeared in testimony. Cousin Samuel Emlen laid before the Meeting his religious concern once more to visit the brethren in some parts of Europe. If he goes, it will, I think, be the sixth time he hath crossed the Atlantic Ocean.

4th Day, 21*st*.—Found myself rather indisposed the fore-part of the day. Afternoon, finding myself better, went out to see a friend.

5th Day, 22*d*.—It proved very sharp to-day, especially towards night. Well for those who have bread in their own houses, comparatively speaking. At brother Joshua's in the evening.

6th Day, 23*d*.—Read, wrote, and walked for my health, to which I think walking is particularly beneficial. Paid a visit to Cousin Thomas Scattergood's family, in company with my wife.

7th Day, 24*th*.—Seasonable for what is called Christmas Eve, being clear and cold.

1st Day, 25*th*.—This being accounted the anniversary of our Blessed Saviour's birth, was a very fine pleasant day, and the streets very lively with people of various denominations resorting to their different places of Worship. Was at our own Meeting, as usual, and hope I received some benefit.

2d Day, 26*th*.—The weather continuing fine, I walked a good deal, about my private affairs, having in contemplation the building of some tenements on a vacant piece of ground I have yet remaining.

3d Day, 27*th*.—At our Monthly Meeting, where we had the company of our European Friends, after which they dined with us, and in the evening several others of our valued friends came in, and added to our satisfaction.

Our good Women had, both of them, something to communicate by way of exhortation, all of which was in the encouraging line, particularly to my dear wife and Johnny.

4th Day, 28th.—The fine weather holds yet. In the evening went out to see a friend.

5th Day, 29th.—At High Street Meeting, Hugh Judge, from Wilmington, and several other Friends appeared in testimony.

To-day I went to see a fine young African lion, which was an unusual sight here, (tho' I have, many years ago, seen a lioness). He was very tame, and appeared to know his keeper.

He was of a light dun colour, and about 3 feet high, to the top of his shoulders; he was not, they said, near to his growth, having but little mane; his fore-feet and claws were exceedingly strong, and he had a very lively, majestic presence.

Great are the works of the Almighty Creator— which every part of His animate (as well as inanimate) Creation loudly proclaim to the thoughful, sensible mind.

From a deep conviction of our weakness and impotence, and His inconceivable power and wisdom, the humble soul is often led to reverence and adore His infinite perfections, at least so far as they are manifested to our finite comprehension.

In the evening walked out to see a friend.

6th Day, 30th.—Not much change in the weather. One of our European Friends' fine wagon horses got into a hole in the stable where they were kept, and kicked and bruised himself to death. This must occasion them some concern and disappointment, as he had been a gentle, useful creature to them for many months past; and Jane Watson drove him mostly, or altogether, herself.

7th Day, 31*st*.—The year ends with a fine, clear day, cold and seasonable.

I have now completed one year of my Diary, and I am not discouraged as yet from continuing it a little longer, if life and health should be vouchsafed, tho' I find it requires some care and attention, as well as labour in writing.

However, if my dear children, on looking over it hereafter, when I am gone, should pick out of it any little hints or observations that may have a tendency to encourage them in a virtuous course, my end and intention will be answered.

For, I often feel the force of parental affection towards them, attended with anxious solicitude for their preservation from the evils which abound in this world, and may say, from long experience, that *we are unable to preserve ourselves*, and are wholly dependent on the bounty and mercy of our adorable Creator.

Let us, then, unitedly look up unto Him for counsel and direction in our movements and steppings along; acknowledge Him in the whole tenor of our conduct and deportment amongst men.

In a word, make His Divine and Holy Law the rule of our lives. We shall then know an improvement in grace, and the gifts of the Holy Spirit.

Let us strive to adorn our Christian profession by our lives, and witness, through the Lord's favour, true happiness in death, when it shall please Him to send the undeniable messenger to summon us from the troubles of time to the joys of eternity.

END OF 1791.

The First Day of the New Year, 1792.

Let me Prefer this Humble Prayer:

O, Thou Great Preserver of Men, whose mercy and goodness have thus far protected me through life; Thou hast been a Parent in the room of those Thou wast pleased to remove from me in the morning of my days; defending me from the temptations of my soul's enemies; and continuing a living hunger and thirst after the Bread and Water of Life; be pleased yet, in Thy great mercy, to be near to me, and conduct me through the remainder of my time in this world in Thy holy fear; that so, when it may please Thee to put a period to my days, I may be of the number of Thy ransomed ones, who through the blessed Atonement made by our Holy Redeemer, may be cleansed from all unrighteousness, and made meet for Thy pure and holy Kingdom.

Gracious Father, as Thou hast been with me, so look down upon my endeared help-meet and tender offspring; make them more and more acquainted with Thy Holy Truth, and preserve them from the evils of the world; that so when our day's work is finished, we may unite in Hallelujahs to Thy Great Name.

1st Day, *1st of First month.*—The year comes in with rain, the morning being very wet and cold. Attended three Meetings, to a degree of comfort and satisfaction.

2d Day, *2d.*—Had the company of several friends from the country, who spent great part of the day with us. Also, our dear aged Mother Elliott, whose eyesight seems nearly gone. She expects to spend a few days with us.

3d Day, *3d.*—At our own Week-day Meeting, after which the adjournment of our Monthly Meeting was held. Weather dull and very damp.

4th Day, *4th.*—Cleared away and was fine, so that the shipping passed up and down the Delaware.

5th Day, *5th.*—At Week-day Meeting, High St. Our Friend M. Ridgway was remarkably close in her testimony, especially to those of the foremost rank. No doubt there is too much unsoundness amongst the members of our Religious Community in this city, which requires so much exercising labour to the honest, devoted servants.

The truth certainly is, that many of us of the present generation are Quakers by education. We have been born so, or at least of parents of that name, and brought up as such, but it may too justly be feared

who I long to see I Remain thy loveing mother Annabella Elliott

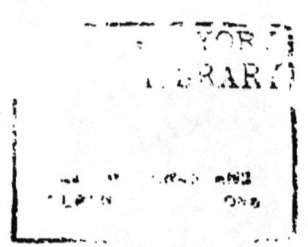

that many have never known the sanctifying operations of the Divine Word, to divide the precious from the vile, or the natural fleshly part from that spiritual part, in and by which alone the Divine Will can be done and performed by us poor weak creatures.

Hence many are (and long continue) in a dwarfish, unfeeling, and almost senseless state, as to the real Life of Religion; and so their tender offspring, educated in the same loose and indifferent way, are often *but nominal* professors.

Another main hindrance to a religious progress is the over-eager pursuit of riches and worldly honour, which too often choke the good seed and render it unfruitful.

May we all profit by the repeated calls of a merciful and compassionate Father, who most certainly wills our present and everlasting happiness, is my sincere desire for myself and others.

6th Day, 6th.—Wrote considerably in my collection.

7th Day, 7th.—Snow, and very cold withal.

1st Day, 8th.—Attended three Meetings, and I hope not altogether in vain.

2d Day, 9th.—Rode a few miles over Schuylkill about some Meeting business. Found the road very rough, and the air excedingly sharp.

3d Day, 10th. — Attended Week-day Meeting, which was silent. Called to see a friend in the afternoon. Wrote in my collection, after-part of the day, and read the Holy Scripture—which, I often find, sweetens the mind, and is a help to keeping it in a peaceful, reverent frame, beyond all other books.

Catharine Greenleaf taken suddenly with something like a paralytic or apopletic stroke, which much surprised her near connections. Mother Elliott went home to brother John's to-day.

4th Day, 11*th.*—This morning the Delaware was frozen over pretty strong, so that the young people ventured on it in considerable numbers. The sharpness of the air kept me and my good wife mostly in-doors—finding a warm house and fireside the most comfortable place. May we be sufficiently thankful for the mercies daily received.

5th Day, 12*th.*—Attended High Street Meeting, where but little was said vocally. Nancy Russel and several others dined, and spent the afternoon with us. In the evening it became what is called intensely cold, with snow 7 or 8 inches deep. Wind easterly; consequently dangerous for vessels on the coast, whom I frequently think of at such times.

6th Day, 13*th.*—Suitable weather for this season. The grain being protected from the severity of the frost, by the covering of snow, is a favourable circumstance.

Very lively about the streets with the sleighs. The bells, which by a late ordinance the horses are compelled to wear—or at least their owners to put on them—make it now much safer for foot passengers than formerly.

7th Day, 14*th.*—Spent the day mostly at home, where I can always find agreeable employment; but, lest it should become burdensome, I vary it—which I find to be not only agreeable but useful. Sometimes I write, either copying or inditing; sometimes read the writings of others, of which there is indeed great store—a great deal, however, is unprofitable, if not hurtful.

Sometimes I split wood, or clear the snow out of my yard, or at least throw it on the border. Sometimes I walk at the back of the town, or in the best part of the streets, when the weather is not inviting to go further.

Sometimes I call to see my friends, and make a point of attending our own, and sometimes go to other Meetings. Thus I am greatly favoured.

I should have mentioned, that in the Summer season I sometimes do a little with my carpenter's tools, or drive a nail here and there. I have also a good deal of work to train, and tend, and dress my vines and flower pots, and my tubs with orange trees.

Add to all this, I am sometimes engaged about little services for the Society; and my small estate is divided among a great many hands, so that I have something to do to attend to them all in season.

Some Wise Men may think these remarks rather trifling, yet perhaps they may hereafter have their use; if so, it's not very material what people say—if we do nothing that's evil or reproachful.

1*st Day*, 15*th*.—At Meeting thrice. Afternoon to see a friend. Weather clear and cold.

2*d Day*, 16*th*.—A fine, wholesome morning;—such weather, I believe, conduces to the health of the inhabitants, as we hear of but few indisposed within the circle of our acquaintance, it being a time of pretty general health.

Yet, as the inhabitants are numerous, most days some drop off. Owen Jones' sister Martha buried to-day, being an antient Friend.

3d Day, 17*th*.—Last night and this morning had a distressing fit of the headache, which continued 'till evening, and deprived me of appetite and outward comfort. I have this consolation, that I am of the mind it may be of use in preventing some other disorder from being introduced into my weak frame. Several friends called in, as I was not at Meeting, as common. In the evening I grew better.

4*th Day*, 18*th*.—This was a dull morning, and proved a snowy day. The snow continued 'till it became deep, attended with severe cold wind.

5*th Day*, 19*th*.—A fine, clear morning, tho' excessively sharp; the wind high and blustering, from the north-west.

Sleighing is now perfectly good, for those who are fond of it. For my part, I had rather be quiet, and excused from such jumbling exercise or diversion. However, for those who travel on real business, or to supply the calls of necessary business, I think it an eligible way of travelling.

Attended High Street Meeting, and in the evening went to see a friend. Felt rather better than common to-day, as to health and spirits.

6*th Day*, 20*th*.—Attended a committee. Wrote in my collection, and read occasionally; so the time passed peacefully, and perhaps as much to our satisfaction, as can reasonably be expected in this imperfect state.

7*th Day*, 21*st*.—Employed much as yesterday.

1st Day, 22*d*.—An addition to the snow on the ground by a considerable fall in the night—so that it was with some difficulty we got to Meeting, which was smaller than usual to-day. The air is now excessively keen.

Sarah Mifflin, (widow of Jonathan Mifflin,) an antient Friend, of four-score, deceased.

So it is, that sooner or later, the time of our pilgrimage here is finished, and we cease, as to bodily presence. Nevertheless, if through infinite mercy, we are preserved by the Divine Power in the integrity and simplicity, we shall be of the accepted.

2d Day, 23*d*.—The weather continues cold, but seasonable. Several sudden deaths about this time. One very remarkable, of a neighbour of the name of Thomas Myers, about 28 years of age, who just before, in apparent health, with his child on his knee, said to his wife he felt poorly, desiring her to take the baby, then falling to the floor, 'tis said, expired in less than ten minutes. Such a vapour is life.

3d Day, 24*th*.—Monthly Meeting day. Also, an adjournment in the afternoon, which held late in the evening.

4th Day, 25*th*.—*5th Day*, 26*th*.—*6th Day*, 27*th*.—The weather moderated, tho' the river continues strongly bound in icy chains, and carriages and sleds with wood are hourly passing, so that we may be said to have a natural bridge for a little season.

Joseph Saunders deceased; also, Dr. Smith suddenly; likewise Dubree's black man, Ishmael, an honest creature, whom I have known many years.

7th Day, 28*th*.—Found engagements of various sorts at home, and the old saying frequently verified, that every day brings its work—and indeed so it does to those who have families.

1st Day, 29*th*.—Attended three Meetings, tho' through some difficulty on account of the weather.

2d Day, 30*th*.—*3d Day*, 31*st*.—The poor boy before mentioned, named William Dillon, was arraigned and tried at the Supreme Court, for setting fire, wilfully and designedly, to several buildings.

He had confessed his guilt to several before his trial, but, as he retracted, the jury did not see fit to convict him upon that ground alone.

There not being sufficient evidence beside, he was acquitted of the crime of arson, which would have touched his life, and found guilty upon another indictment of perjury, he was sentenced to several years hard labour.

4th Day, 1*st of Second month*.—Had the headache to-day, which generally disqualifies me for any useful exertion.

5th Day, 2*d*.—At High Street Meeting, where we were invited to the burial of our friend John Head. He was near 70, and by a life of care and frugality, and a blessing upon his endeavours, had gathered an abundance of what is called wealth, and I hope, with an unblemished character.

I have often thought that *great* earthly riches are no real advantage to our posterity; for they oftentimes elevate the minds of the young and inexperienced, and divert or discourage the work of true religion upon the mind.

Keeping it aloof from that deep and weighty sense of the importance of our *being* in this probationary state, and the necessity of placing our affections on things above, in order to be fitted and prepared for a rest in the Day of Trouble, when our pilgrimage through time and the trials of mortality are at an end.

6*th Day*, 3*d*.—Walked to the stone quarry at the upper ferry, about some stone for my intended building. I find it useful and conducive to health, now and then to take a little exercise this way, but yet it may be overdone; that is exercise beyond the bodily powers, which of course destroys the benefit expected or desired.

7*th Day*, 4*th*.—Morning dull, but cleared away, and proved moderate towards evening. I think the time in Winter seems to pass swifter than in Summer, and perhaps various reasons may be assigned why it is so.

I have made another remark or observation sometimes, that in advanced life the years appear to roll round quicker than in youth. This also, may, I think, be easily accounted for.

I am sensible variety of circumstances have great effect, according to our situations and our advantages as to our stations in the world, so that we have different prospects and sentiments at different periods of our lives.

But, be these what they may, *resignation* to the Divine Will is a most happy, tho' I well know, a difficult attainment. This will, in a good measure, reconcile us to our allotments, calm the mind in affliction, and preserve it from too great elevation in prosperity, knowing everything mutable is unstable.

Let us then, dear children, labour after this great and necessary virtue; and the nearer we attain to it, the more we shall experience its excellency as an antidote against the evils of human life, or what may appear to us as such.

I believe we are often mistaken in our apprehensions in that respect, and that blessings are sometimes dispensed to us in disguise; for the dispensations of Unerring Wisdom are unsearchable, yet always in mercy and love to those who truly fear Him, and who are, in uprightness and sincerity, desirous to serve Him with all the strength and ability afforded.

1*st Day*, 5*th*.—At Meeting three times, as usual. How much owest thou unto thy Lord, was the language of my heart, for the continuation of unmerited blessings, both outward and inward:—health to myself and my family, a sufficiency of temporal things, peace and plenty on every hand. May my heart be grateful and thankful, ever remembering that all is derived from Him who is the source of bounty and perfection.

2*d Day*, 6*th*.—Was at our Quarterly Meeting, which went through their business at two sittings. Our North Meeting House accommodated us pretty well, this being the first Quarterly Meeting held there. Samuel Emlen and Sarah Harrison's religious concerns for England were united with, and sanctioned by endorsements on their certificates severally.

3*d Day*, 7*th*.—Was Youth's Meeting in course, but I did not attend it, my brother-in-law Isaac Gray being ill, and judged to be near his end in this world. Towards evening it set in for a heavy snow storm.

4th Day, 8*th*.—Snow eight or more inches deep on a level, and tho' the weather appeared so very winter-like, our valued Friends, M. Ridgway and Jane Watson, left the city with a view to visit some Meetings in Chester County and Delaware State. I. G. grows weaker. My wife stays with her sister altogether, in this her time of trial.

5*th Day*, 9*th*.—Another fall of snow in the night. I was at High Street Meeting, which was favoured with some instructive ministry through our Friend George Dillwyn.

The river is so firm that loaded carriages pass with confidence. Wood, $4.00 to $6.00 a cord, and plenty from both Jersey and Pennsylvania sides.

6*th Day*, 10*th*.—Real winter, in its proper season.

7*th Day*, 11*th*.—Brother Isaac takes little or no sustenance, or notice of any person or thing that passes —lying in one position mostly. But we hope he is favoured with his senses in these awful moments, being very still and quiet.

1*st Day*, 12*th*.—Between 12 and 1 last night my brother-in-law, Isaac Gray, departed this life. He was favoured with an easy passage, to outward appearance, without that agony which often attends these mortal tabernacles.

The greater part of his life he was well respected, and was considered as a man of parts and learning, having served in the Assembly several years. He was upwards of 20 years in a married state; he had one daughter, who lived but a few minutes. He was aged near 44 years.

2d Day, 13*th*.—More snow fell.

3d Day, 14*th*.—Preparative Meeting, but did not attend it, on account of my brother-in-law's decease.

4th Day, 15*th*.—This afternoon my brother-in-law Isaac Gray was interred in the north-west corner of Friends' burial ground. The funeral was respectfully attended by many relations and former acquaintance. It was a cold day, and much snow on the ground.

5th Day, 16*th*.—Attended High Street Meeting. Afternoon employed in writing. I think Solomon tells us that there is a time for every purpose, and much, no doubt, depends upon the well timing of almost every concern and undertaking in life; for very many well-laid plans and purposes have failed on account of their being injudiciously timed.

This observation of the wisest of men may be applied both to temporals and spirituals, and also to things of lesser as well as greater magnitude and importance. I have often realized the assertion in the lines of experience.

There is another thing which conduces much to the success of even our honest enterprises; that is, after our plans are well laid and well timed, then be resolute and steady in the execution, and, trusting to Divine help, they are seldom abortive.

6th Day, 17*th*.—*7th Day*, 18*th*.—These two days I spent mostly in writing, reading, and some calls among my friends.

1st Day, 19*th*.—At three Meetings, agreeable to my usual custom when in health.

2d Day, 20*th*.—The weather continues very cold. Much snow on the ground, and it may be said with truth, that we have had a severe winter thus far—the river having been frozen over now about six weeks, the greater part of which time loaded carriages have passed and repassed daily. Much wood has come to the city from the Jersey shore above and below this place.

3d Day, 21*st*.—At Monthly Meeting, which, at two sittings, went through their business, in about seven hours.

4th Day, 22*d*.—Walked nearly to Schuylkill, about stone for my intended building, and found it cold and sloppy.

5th Day, 23*d*.—Attended High Street Meeting, where several Friends were concerned in testimony. James Cresson and George Dillwyn were two of the number.

6th Day, 24*th*.—*7th Day*, 25*th*.—The weather now moderates as the sun gathers strength, and it affords a pleasure to the mind to have indications of the approach of spring, after being so long inured to the boisterous blasts of the north winds.

How infinitely and stupendously powerful is the Supreme Creator, who made and supports the universe with such inconceivable wisdom and order, that every part of the mighty whole is preserved and maintained in its proper place and station, and is subservient to the Great Maker's purpose. He is always operating powerfully (tho' sometimes out of sight,) in upholding both the visible and invisible creation.

There is great diversity in the climates of the different parts of the globe we inhabit, and the Zones are divided into one Torrid or Burning Zone, two Temperate, and two Frigid or Frozen Zones.

Of these, we are situated in one of the Temperate Zones. Our climate is variable, but this, according to my apprehension, makes it the more agreeable. For the contrast between heat and cold has with me a tendency to make the return of spring more welcome after the winter's cold; and the approach of winter after the summer's heat, serves to brace and strengthen our relaxed frames after the warm season has passed. So that we have every reason to be contented and thankful for our allotment on this ball of earth.

For, if we were in a situation so mild as to be unacquainted with frost, or so severe as that of Greenland and other northern regions, where there is but little heat or warmth, it would, in my opinion, be more unpleasant than to have our present changes.

However, I do not undertake to determine for others, as I am aware that mankind in general give the preference to their native country.

This love of country has a powerful tendency to bind us to the soil that gave us birth. No doubt it was put into our hearts in wisdom infinite, in order that the human race should be dispersed and divided on the surface of the globe, and furnished with the means of subsistence, during the little span of time that is afforded them for the great purpose of rendering them fit inhabitants for the far better world to come, where, we are taught to believe, all will be fixed and unalterable.

1st Day, 26*th*.—Cloudy, with rain. Attended Meeting as usual.

2d Day, 27*th*.—Much rain in the night, but the river keeps firm.

3d Day, 28*th*.—At Meeting; afterwards on Society business. John Norris buried, who was killed by a fall from a scaffold.

4th Day, 29*th*.—Attended the funeral of Stanton Dorsey, aged about 24. He was grandson of that worthy, Daniel Stanton; but alas, it matters not to whom we are related, or who were our progenitors! If we do not well ourselves, we cannot expect to be Divinely approved. This youth, unhappily, took, early in life, to bad courses, in which he persevered, so as 'tis too probable he shortened his days by his evil conduct.

O, ever to be lamented folly! that neither the affectionate entreaties of our nearest friends, the loss of health and reputation, and above all, the remonstrances and convictions of the holy, unflattering Witness for Truth in our own breasts, can prevail, so as to induce those simple ones to forsake the paths of death and destruction, and turn to the Lord whilst the door of mercy remains standing open; for if ever it is eternally shut against us, woe indeed, must be our portion.

However, I attempt not to decide on the state of this poor young man. He had a long space of sickness and bodily weakness, which may be acccounted a favour; and if he made a proper use and improvement thereof, we know that the Lord sustains the adorable character of Infinite in Mercy and Goodness towards the truly penitent in heart.

5th Day, 1*st of Third month.*—This we call the first Spring day, and a pleasant one it is. Neighbour Robinson began his new building near my dwelling.

Was much indisposed with the sick headache. May be it is a mercy to keep me from resting in any of the enjoyments here below.

For, as I am favoured to have a comfortable share of outward things without much labour, if I had not some alloy, I see there is danger of cleaving too close to earth and lower objects, and neglecting the great and momentous work, which is so important to all.

6th Day, 2*d.*—Moderate, and a good deal spring-like, 'tho the icy chains of winter's piercing cold yet bind the Delaware and Schuylkill.

7th Day, 3*d.*—Variously employed, and I hope not unprofitably. I meditated upon the shortness and uncertainty of earthly goods; their inability to satisfy the immortal part, which at times is favoured to see and contemplate the end of all things here as swiftly approaching with resistless force. O, for a preparation for a better inheritance than this world can give to any of its most devoted sons.

1*st Day,* 4*th.*—At Meeting thrice, where we were favoured with the right sort of preaching.

2*d Day,* 5*th.*—The morning was ushered in with thunder and lightning—very awful, as well as uncommon, at this season. Much rain accompanied it.— However, it continues cold. River not broken up.

3*d Day,* 6*th.*—Attended our Week-day Meeting, at which we heard the voice of our valued Friend

Thomas Scattergood, who lately returned from a six weeks religious visit to some Meetings in Jersey.

George Dillwyn also appeared, and we may allow it was an edifying time. Attended a Committee on Society business. In the evening was also employed in the same way.

4th Day, *7th*.—Was indisposed with the sick headache—very poorly indeed. Nothing but patience will do any good.

5th Day, *8th*.— Better. In the afternoon it rained and snowed, and was very stormy. However, I got to a Committee at Fourth Street House. Ice in the river begins to move.

6th Day, *9th*.—Clear morning; the snow 3 or 4 inches deep, but was mostly gone by night. Attended a Committee on Meeting business in the afternoon. Some small craft, 'tis said, begin to move on the river.

7th Day, *10th*.—A rainy morning, and proved a thorough wet day, which, in all likelihood, will open the navigation. There is a considerable freshet in the Delaware. Kept mostly within doors, and found agreeable employment.

1st Day, *11th*.—At Meeting, as usual.

2d Day, *12th*.—Cool and blustering, like March. Tradesmen in the building way seem to get in motion, and 'tis expected that many good houses will go on this season. Materials and workmanship, consequently, rate high.

3d Day, *13th*.—Attended Week-day Meeting and an appointment. Then some necessary matters of a private nature. I find I am generally more fit to conduct my worldly business when my mind is seasoned at a good Meeting, by getting as near as possible to the Inward Principle, and true place of waiting, and as it were, feeling my way through the thorns and briers of a delusive world, which often hangs out false colours to deceive the simple and captivate the unguarded.

Let us, therefore, maintain the spiritual watch, my dear children, for we are no longer safe than while we are on our guard against the Grand Enemy of souls.

4th Day, 14th.—*5th Day*, 15th.—Much taken up about my new building. The weather coarse and blustering. A cold rain, with snow, came on towards evening of Fifth-day.

About fifty Indians came to town; said to be of the Six Nations. How earnestly is it to be desired that they may be instrumental in bringing about a peace with their country-folks to the Westward, where so much blood hath been lately shed.

Mother Elliott came to spend a few days with us.

6th Day, 16th.—Snow fell to a considerable depth, but soon disappeared. Afternoon attended a Committee. Am favoured to feel pretty well in health.

7th Day, 17th.—A remarkably fine day, which I filled up with various avocations.

How swiftly time passes; daily numbering many to a state of everlasting fixedness. Of what importance, then, is it to be in a condition to render an account of our stewardship.

May I bear this consideration ever in mind, and regulate my conduct, not upon the things of time, but as a probationer for eternity, which may most properly be called our home, and this life but as a prelude or passage to the awful, all-interesting, after scene.

1st Day, 18*th*.—Attended three Meetings. Our European Women Friends, M. Ridgway and Jane Watson, came to town yesterday, after spending a few weeks among the Meetings in Chester County. They represent the badness of the roads as exceeding any they ever saw.

2d Day, 19*th*.—The masons began to lay stone in my new building. At Overseer's Meeting in the afternoon. Evening, to see a friend.

3d Day, 20*th*.—Rain in the night. Was detained from Meeting, much against my inclination.

4th Day, 21*st*.—In the afternoon was a funeral in the ground opposite our door, of an Indian, one of the company who lately arrived from the back country. Several thousand spectators attended, from motives of curiosity, and were very disorderly, much, I think, to the discredit of our city.

5th Day, 22*d*.—At High Street Meeting, where our European Women Friends were acceptably heard in public testimony.

We are informed of the decease of David Deshler, an antient Friend of German descent; also, Hannah, the widow of Joseph Morris, a meek-spirited, good woman, I think, if there be any such.

In the evening visited two families, with several other Friends, by appointment.

6th Day, 23*d*.—Warm for the season, and showery. Got out my trees, which have been housed all winter, in order that they may be refreshed with the rain. I likewise uncovered my grape vines.

7th Day, 24*th*.—Our Spring Meeting begins to-day, but it must be with difficulty country Friends get to town, the roads are so miry. A wet day.

1st Day, 25*th*.—The public service of this day was, I hope, truly edifying unto many. Had the satisfaction of some of our Friends' company.

2d Day, 26*th*.—A cool, uncomfortable day, both damp and wet, which affects my poor weak frame. Several of our family were also affected with colds.

3d Day, 27*th*.—It cleared away fine and pleasant. Spring Meeting now concludes. Samuel Emlen and Sarah Harrison set at liberty to proceed on their religious visit to Europe; John Pemberton don't go yet. Our European Friends had certificates for their return to their native country. A good deal taken up with worldly concerns.

4th Day, 28*th*.—The warmest day we have had this Spring, which made the buds shoot fast. The first day that I have noticed the martins. Got up some of our vines.

Mother Hopkins and several young people came to visit us. Was poorly in the evening, with my sick headache.

My mind was solidly impressed with the uncertainty of our time here in this world, and the great importance of a preparation for a state of everlasting fixidness. May I properly improve the few remaining days of my allotted span, so that I may, through Infinite Goodness and Mercy, finish well when the end comes, is my sincere labour and prayer to the God of my life.

5th Day, 29*th*.—6*th Day*, 30*th*.—Much engaged about earthly things, and as I apprehended, necessarily so. However, I am persuaded that *too great* an abundance is an entanglement in our progress towards the Holy City; and tho' we who have families cannot shake off such engagements altogether, let us endeavour to keep them as much under rule as possible.

7*th Day*, 31*st*.—Poorly in health;—something of a fever and humour in my head and face, attended with a pain in my bones.

1*st Day*, 1*st of Fourth month*.—At Meeting thrice, being a little better.

2*d Day*, 2*d*.—My head and hands full of worldly cares. How do I desire ardently, to keep the great point steadily in view, and all outward things subservient thereto.

3*d Day*, 3*d*.—Adjournment of the Monthly Meeting.

When I came home was acquainted with an unpleasant occurrence, by the bursting of a well near one I was causing to be dug, by which one of the workmen was in danger of his life. These things sometimes will happen to those concerned in building.

4*th Day*, 4*th*.—Taken up endeavouring to remedy the cross occurrence which happened yesterday in our well, which, with much exercise and difficulty, we accomplished. We are in hopes, tho' the prospect at first was gloomy, and judged by some to be past remedy, that it may eventually be no great detriment.

5*th Day*, 5*th*.—Had a blister put upon my back, for a complaint in my ear.

6th Day, 6*th.*—The blister, according to present appearances, has had a good effect. However, was a good deal indisposed, and kept house altogether.

7th Day, 7*th.*—Poorly in the morning, but better in the after part of the day. Planted a couple more new vines from Slaughter's Garden, which I believe to be of a good kind.

Afternoon attended the burial of Robert Hudson, a young man about 30, who had been wild and extravagant in his conduct. Yet some, who visited him on his sick-bed, were led to hope favour and mercy were extended, through unfeigned repentance.

1st Day, 8*th.*—About the first week in this month the day breaks about 5 o'clock, and the evening shuts in about 7. My daily practice of rising early, gives me occasion to make this observation. The mornings and evenings, however, are cool, tho' the noon is warm and pleasant.

My orange trees a good deal pinched, but I allow I set them out too soon. In general, the middle of the Fourth month is quite early enough.

2d Day, 9*th.*—Went on with our building, and also some repairs which I have in hand. It is a fine thing to do things in proper season.

3d Day, 10*th.*—At the adjournment of Monthly Meeting, William Savery proposed his concern to go to Virginia, and Thomas Scattergood to Carolina and probably Georgia. Was much distressed with the uneasiness of my blister, now healing, which occasioned me to sit this long Meeting with much difficulty. However, in the afternoon I pushed out again, and walked nearly to Schuylkill, after some stone for my building.

4th Day, 11*th*.—A poor night, and also an uneasy day with my blister. I find it a sore thing from first to last; but yet it seems to have removed, in a great measure, the complaint in my ear, and perhaps may help my headache. A wet day.

5th Day, 12*th*.—At High Street Meeting, Amos Gregg and Ann Maris married. George Dillwyn appeared, also Lydia Starr, and both, I thought, to satisfaction.

6th Day, 13*th*.—*7th Day*, 14*th*.—Having a difficult job in hand, I was much taken up in procuring materials and contriving for the best.

1st Day, 15*th*.—A remarkable day of favour at each of the three Meetings. How much owest thou unto thy Lord, was the query; and it may be made with as much truth in our day as formerly.

2d Day, 16*th*.—As busy as well could be, and I esteem it a great favour. My health is in good measure preserved, so as not to be disabled from attending on the workmen.

3d Day, 17*th*.—Preparative Meeting, and a great deal of business. Rainy in the afternoon, and warm.

4th Day, 18*th*.—Preserved in tolerable health, which I account a great mercy.

5th Day, 19*th*.—Employed as yesterday. Got along peaceably, and to my satisfaction. It is by degrees, and through perseverance and patience, we can accomplish any considerable undertaking.

6th Day, 20*th*.—Proved a rainy morning, which drove us from our work. The spring has been generally unfavourable for building and brick-making. Doubtless all is ordered in Unerring Wisdom—for, on other accounts, as to grass and vegetation, it is a fine season.

On the produce of the ground man chiefly depends for his subsistence—so 'tis our duty to be thankful and contented with the various dispensations meted out to us, dependent as we are upon Divine Bounty.

7th Day, 21*st*.—Wet and very wet, which interrupts our progress. However, it will have its use in the creation, and when the sun again dispenses its genial heat and warmth, will bring forward the produce of the earth with redoubled force.

Better of my cold and other complaints. I have been taking dandelion juice in the morning fasting—and apply the bark, say Jesuit's bark, to the crown of my head, which has been recommended for my common complaint.

Attended the burial of an Indian, (one of those who came to this city some time ago,) called the Big Tree. He was buried in Friends' ground, at the request of his companions, and many Friends were present.

A discourse was made by their Missionary or Minister in the Indian language, which, though I could not understand, had something pleasing in it. Our Friend George Dillwyn spoke afterwards, and the funeral was conducted with solemnity. About 36 Indians followed the deceased, and their countenances were remarkably solid and grave. A wet, dripping day.

1*st Day*, 22*d*.—Was favoured to be well enough to be at three Meetings.

2*d Day*, 23*d*.—Fully employed about necessary occasions.

3d Day, 24*th*.—Monthly Meeting. Our Friends W. Savery and Thomas Scattergood's certificates prepared and signed—the first for Virginia—the latter for Carolina. Did some writing to send abroad.

4th Day, 25*th*.—Was about home most part of the day, being cumbered about many things. O that I may not forget or neglect the one thing *only* needful, in a comparative sense, with all others.

5th Day, 26*th*.—A dull day, but I pressed through to Meeting.

6th Day, 27*th*.—Went on with my temporal matters pretty well. We have always something or other to try our patience, but in the right sort of confidence we possess our minds, and if our hearts are upright, we are generally helped along, though at times beset on every hand with difficulties.

7th Day, 28*th*.—Mother Elliott on a visit at our house for a few days; Sister Gray also with her.—Dull and drizzly, but felt pretty well. Time makes a steady progress, and whether we employ it well or ill, we are accountable for its use or abuse.

How important is life!—how awful is death! If one day on a sick-bed appears so invaluable, how necessary to put our talent or talents to usury; that so, on a final reckoning, we may not be amazed or confounded with the sentence of the slothful servant.

1st Day, 29*th*.—A severe spell of the sick headache, which confined me to the bed most of the day. It was a cross not to be able to go to the Meeting—but there was no remedy but patience and submission. At morning Meeting William Savery, I am told, had the public service, being about leaving us for a season.

I hear Job Scott, an eminent Minister of Providence, New England, has laid his concern for Europe before the Meeting he belongs to. It was what I expected when in those parts last summer, and now seems likely to take place, I trust, in due time.

2d Day, 30*th*.—Growing weather, tho' it is not allowed to be a forward spring. Yet I hope we may be favoured with a good fruit year, as the blossoms are abundant. However, we may yet have some frosty mornings, which may disappoint our wishes.

3d Day, 1*st of Fifth month*.—May Day—a high day among the milk-maids in London, as 'tis said, when they go about the streets with garlands of flowers.

The custom of setting up May Poles on this day here, which has been annually practised for many years past, seems much to decline—hardly any to be seen. Building, in most parts of the city goes on with great spirit.

4th Day, 2*d*.—Markets high; and wood also:—Oak, 22*s*. 6*d*. a price not usual at this season.

5th Day, 3*d*.—At Market or High Street Meeting. Much taken up afterwards about various concerns.

6th Day, 4*th*.—Rainy, but found employment. Mary Newport, deceased.

7th Day, 5*th*.—A busy day. Almost overdid the matter for I had a heavy fit of my headache, which I have reason to think is frequently brought on by over-fatigue. It continued bad through the night. I may safely say I have been for 30 years a patient sufferer by this trying complaint, and have never found any application or medicine effectual for removing it, therefore am compelled to submit to it as a part of the portion of human evil dispensed to all the sons of Adam.

1*st Day*, 6*th*.—At morning Meeting several savory testimonies were delivered; also, a prayer or two.

2*d Day*, 7*th*.—Our Quarterly Meeting was held (being the second time) in the North Meeting House, to good satisfaction.

3*d Day*, 8*th*.—Attended a Committee on the service of the Quarterly Meeting; also, to some private affairs, having several irons in the fire, and not willing either of them should burn for want of care.

4*th Day*, 9*th*.—Proceeded with our building to satisfaction, the weather being fine and suitable for our purpose. Bought 8 or 9 cords of hickory, at 25*s*. which is counted low.

5*th Day*, 10*th*.—To appearance, settled fine weather. Another fit of my usual complaint.

6*th Day*, 11*th*.—A fine, fair morn. Nature, rejoicing in the bounty of the Great Creator, now putting on her gayest robes; the fields luxuriant; the animal creation in vigour and high health—O, that we may not abuse them—the generous horse particularly, the sportive lamb, the profitable cow, the useful ox—all contribute to supply the wants and promote the welfare of man, whose heart should expand with love and gratitude to the bountiful and beneficent Author of every blessing.

The warmest day this season; no coming near the fire with comfort. I pity the brick-layer's labourers, panting among the lime-dust.

7*th Day*, 12*th*.—A busy day, with some interruptions. However, got along reasonably well.

1st Day, 13*th*.—At three Meetings, which were mostly silent. The weather being very warm, has a natural tendency to relax weak frames. Wrote a letter in the evening to a friend.

2d Day, 14*th*.—Got forward with our business.

3d Day, 15*th*.—A favoured Meeting, after which the Preparative Meeting was held.

4th Day, 16*th*.—Wet. Got a wrench or strain in the small of my back, which was painful and troublesome. Bled, &c. Being off my legs, could do but little.

5th Day, 17*th*.—Could not attend Meeting. In much pain; towards evening a little relieved. Near night, Mother Elliott and Sister Gray went home to brother John's.

6th Day, 18*th*.—Felt a little on the mending order. We hear of the decease of our valued Friend Samuel Neal, of Ireland, who 'tis said, deceased 27th 2d month last, of a mortification in his foot, about the 65th year of his age.

He, together with Susannah Lightfoot, appeared in Public Testimony at our wedding, about 20 years ago, being then on a religious visit to this country.

7th Day, 19*th*.—Attempted too soon to exert myself, and so got worse of my strain, and was bad indeed—so that I could scarce move without crying out.

1st Day, 20*th*.—Was on the bed most of the day, and could scarce tell whether I mended or not. However, towards night I sat up a little, and a pretty good night followed.

I find we must use endeavours to help ourselves inwardly, as well as outwardly, and put our own shoulders to the wheels, as well as call for assistance from others, and then we may reasonably hope to get along through the variety of ills attendant on our passage through this lower stage of being.

Cousin Thomas Scattergood set off on his journey to Carolina and Georgia.

2d Day, 21*st*.—Felt myself on the mending hand, and very careful I was, not to interrupt nature in her operations to restore strength to my poor frame.—Walked about a little with a staff. Health is the most precious of outward treasures.

3d Day, 22*d*.—Our Monthly Meeting, but I was an absentee, through necessity only, as it would have been imprudent to have attempted to sit a Meeting in my weak state.

4th Day, 23*d*.—Still grew better, but slowly.—Walked out to see how our workmen went on. Used balsam of fir for my strain, which I believe to be a beneficial medicine.

5th Day, 24*th*.—Clear and warm.

6th Day, 25*th*.—Could not say I was well, tho' much better upon the whole. Was favoured to conclude these twenty-four hours to satisfaction.

7th Day, 26*th*.—Employed as usual. A time to labour, and a time to reap the harvest which it is wont to produce. May the blessing from above be added, else all is vanity.

1st Day, 27*th*.—Calm and serene—a sweet day of rest.

2d Day, 28*th*.—Felt bravely in health, for which I desire to be thankful to the Great Author of every blessing.

Several sudden deaths about this time—among others, Mary Garrigues, was at Meeting one day and died before another dawned; an awful instance of the uncertainty of time.

A man sank down and died as he was attending in his shop, and another in the same neighbourhood, after a few hours illness. John Gravenstine, a stout man, to appearance likely to live many years, taken off very suddenly.

So the messenger is commissioned to go from house to house to fulfil the decree of the Highest.— Let us stand in awe, and not sin, for we know not the day nor hour when we may be summoned to a fixed and unalterable state.

3d Day, 29*th*.—At Week-day Meeting, Samuel Noble and Elizabeth Tomkins entered into marriage covenant. The Adjournment of the Monthly Meeting was afterwards held, and the business finished. Performed a little service for the cause's sake, which afforded satisfaction to my mind.

Was out on business the after part of the day, and felt in a good degree comfortable as to my health. My weak frame seems to feel full as well in warm as in cold weather; life being supported by heat and warmth may be the fundamental reason.

The creation now in its vigour since the nights became warm. A noble appearance of crops on the ground.

4*th Day*, 30*th*.—This was a general cleaning and white-washing day, consequently our house was turned upside down, as the saying is. The women part of the family were weary enough by bed-time, and, indeed, I did not need a cradle myself.

5th Day, 31*st*.—Rose before the sun, as I have for many days past, and with my dear Caleb did some work in the yard in the cool part of the morning, that being best for such sort of business, especially for those who are not much inured to labour, for when the sun approaches the meridian it beats us off.

I went to Meeting, and afterwards performed some errands. This proved a very warm day.

In the evening my dear Johnny returned from a little journey to Crosswick's Quarterly Meeting. He was well-pleased with his ride. I felt thankful for his safety and preservation to the Great Preserver.

The thermometer rose to 90 degrees the latter part of this day.

6th Day, 1*st of Sixth month*.—Cloudy, sultry and close. The evening produced a fine shower, which greatly refreshed the face of nature.

Thomas Shute deceased, a poor distressed object, who had for many years been conversant in the school of affliction. He was buried from our neighbour Robinson's being his wife's brother.

Got along with my outward concerns, step by step. Exertion on our part is indispensably necessary, or we cannot expect to attain the desired end.

7th Day, 2*d*.—About 4 o'clock there was a fine soaking shower, which was an addition to the blessing of last night.

The creation may be said to be now in its fullest vigour—everything thriving and pressing towards perfection.

May we imitate the progress of nature, in a spiritual sense, and endeavour to attain the end, the great end, set before the children of men, that is, to finish well, and close the scene of life peacefully, that so death may not have a sting, nor the grave a victory.

Attended the remains of T. Shute to the place appointed for all the living.

Last night our neighbour Roe took a final leave of earth. She was advanced beyond the middle stage of life, had borne a number of children, and been an industrious, careful woman. But many secret sorrows were mingled in her cup, and towards her close she was pressed beyond the powers of nature, so that reason failed, and she groaned out the remains of life to appearance in great agony.

Yet this consolation remains for the upright in heart, that the Lord seeth not as man seeth;—He knoweth all things, and will reward or punish accordingly.

I hope her departed spirit may find acceptance, trusting that, according to the testimony of Holy Writ, she was one of those who had *done what she could*.

1*st Day*, 3*d*.—A dull, warm, growing morning. The creation now in her glory, all vigorous and gay, the sap flowing with uninterrupted force. Fruit and flowers, grain and grass, all spontaneously forming under nature's hand—how or wherefore we know not. But thus much we do know of a certainty, that there must, without any doubt, be a great and supremely powerful First Cause. To Him, then, let us bend the knee of our minds in humble adoration, and render Him the just praise of all His works, which abound with wonder, mystery, and astonishing magnificence.

Whether we contemplate Him in the lowest or highest order of His visible creation—either in the depths of the earth, or the heights of heaven, (the Planetary System, as it is sometimes termed)—all His works exhibit just ground for wonder. How manifold! how grand! how strikingly gracious and bountiful!

Let us, therefore, adore Him, both with tongue and heart, as God over all, supremely worthy of power and majesty, infinite and unutterable, and let us, with the royal Psalmist, say—*"Give unto the Lord, O ye mighty, give unto the Lord glory and strength!"* *"Give unto the Lord the glory due unto his name."* *"Worship the Lord in the beauty of holiness."*

Attended the funeral of our neighbour Roe in the evening, after which went to see a friend or two, and so returned home with my dear wife, and retired to rest.

2d Day, 4*th*.—As the days are now nearly at the longest, at about 4 we have light sufficient for almost any business, and pleasant it is to enjoy the fragrance of the morning dawn, mixed with the sweet gales of odoriferous flowers that perfume the breath of nature at this high period of her strength.

3d Day, 5*th*.—A favoured Meeting. John Evans and Rachel Ridgway married. Very warm day, so as to be, some part of it, quite oppressive.

4th Day, 6*th*.—Close and sultry; rain in the afternoon. Felt pretty well and comfortable. Exercised myself in dressing my vines, and some other little matters. My vines flourish, and look promising.

5th Day, 7th.—Meeting at High Street. Felt low, but composed in mind—viewing human life but as a passing cloud, and everything on this visible theatre terminating with a rapid progress as to those who live and exist at the present moment.

We hear of the assassination of the King of Sweden, one of his officers having shot five balls into his bowels. The Grand Sultan also was in danger of losing his life, by an attempt made upon him at a public assembly. Royalty itself, we experience, is not exempt from calamity, and the long black roll of human woes.

The blacks and mulattoes on the island of Hisspainola, at least on the French side of the island, have made a revolt from their old task-masters—having armed themselves, and being filled with indignation and despair, are carrying fire and sword through the different settlements, in order to recover that personal liberty which, unquestionably, was intended by the Great Author of Nature as a right unalienable to the human species.

It is not, I think, unworthy of remark, that about 300 years ago, Columbus first discovered the island of Hispainola, where the insurrection has taken place, and by the power of the Spanish arms, subdued the natives by devastation and slaughter. Now, in the Divine ordering of events, may perhaps be permitted the restoration of freedom to this oppressed part of mankind, and, if the Lord's good time is arrived, 'tis possible with Him to break the bonds of those who have for many years been held in grievous bondage and captivity, under worse than Egyptian task-masters.

6th Day, 8*th*.—Found enough to keep myself full of employment through this day.

7th Day, 9*th*.—Our workmen have got to the top stone, so we made them welcome, in the evening, to a small repast.

1st Day, 10*th*.—Attended two Meetings. The evening wet, so I kept house, not being very well.

2d Day, 11*th*.—*3d Day*, 12*th*.—Usual engagements, but did not forget Meeting.

4th Day, 13*th*.—*5th Day*, 14*th*.—My hands, as well as head, much employed, besides a good deal of company.

6th Day, 15*th*.—By mercy we stand, if, having done all that is required, we do stand; therefore, not any merit in us, but free grace alone.

7th Day, 16*th*.—Many avocations occurred, but got through with some degree of satisfaction.

1st Day, 17*th*.—Attended Meetings as usual.

2d Day, 18*th*.—*3d Day*, 19*th*.—These two days I was much taken up adjusting my little concerns and preparing for a journey with my dear wife and son Caleb to New York and Long Island.

4th Day, 20*th*.—To-day we left Philadelphia about six in the evening, and after a pleasant run over Delaware, proceded seven miles to Haddonfield.

At Haddonfield I married my first wife, Sarah Hopkins, daughter of Ebenezer and Sarah Hopkins, with whom I lived about two years and four months, when she deceased of a nervous fever, after about two weeks illness, 9th month 12th, 1769, in the 21st year of her age.

Our little daughter Mary, then about 18 months old, lived 'til her ninth year, and died at Philadelphia, 19th 1st month, 1777, of the small pox; a very amiable child, both as to person and temper.

Of her mother, I may also mention that she was a virtuous, discreet, meek-spirited woman, and I had a prospect of much comfort and satisfaction in our union. But He who orders all things in unerring wisdom, permitted it not to be of long duration—in whose appointments I wish ever to be resigned, as much as human frailty will permit.

This was a heavy stroke to me, and was the means of my return to my native city in about six months, with my little daughter.

On the 16th of 4th month, 1772, I formed another connection with my present much-beloved companion, with whom I have now continued 20 years.

Though we have had a large portion of the trials and afflictions attendant upon human life, we may, with great thankfulness and gratitude, acknowledge that hitherto we have been helped in a remarkable manner under and over our various difficulties, which excites to humble confidence in the Great Preserver of men.

We desire to walk before Him in His holy fear, and with dedication of heart to His service, which is the alone safe and peaceful state we can attain to in this world.

At Haddonfield we lodged at Mother Hopkins', and were kindly entertained two nights.

5th Day, 21*st*.—Was at Haddonfield Week-day Meeting, where I had not been for several years before, though I always thought it a pleasant place. Afternoon went over to my brother-in-law John Hopkins, and spent the afternoon agreeably in his family. Had a fine shower of rain in the evening; however, we got home to our lodgings without much inconvenience.

6th Day, 22*d.*—Rose early this morning, with a view of being upon the road by sunrise, as the pleasantest time of travelling at this season, but as it proved a very foggy, damp morning, considering we were none of us very stout, so concluded to stay at our quarters 'til after breakfast, when we got under way, and going through Moorestown, it became very warm after the sun broke out.

Towards noon we reached Mount Holly, a little tired with our warm ride. After dining at Rosell's Tavern, went in to see our kind friend Elizabeth Hatkinson, who invited us to lodge there, which was acceptable, as we had reason to believe our accommodation at the inn would be but indifferent.

Caleb went, after dinner, to the top of the great hill near the town, called the Mount, from which, together with the holly ground adjoining—where the buildings principally stand, the town derives its name. From the top of this mount a noble prospect opens to view, and 'tis said, when the air is clear our city steeples may be discerned. He also went to view the mills and water works, which are worth seeing.

7th Day, 23*d.*—Rain in the fore part of the day induced us to stay 'til afternoon. About 5 we set off for Burlington, a sloppy ride of 7 miles, where we arrived in pretty good time in the evening, and after seeing our horses well taken care of at the tavern, took up our quarters for the night at E. and M. Barker's.

1st *Day*, 24*th*.—Attended Burlington Meeting, forenoon and afternoon. Lydia Hoskins and George Dillwyn exercised their gifts in the Ministry.

Drank tea at John Cox's; viewed Sucky Dillwyn's silk-worms. In the evening called in at several friends' houses, and then retired to rest.

2*d Day*, 25*th*.—Rose early, with an intention of taking a morning ride to our old neighbour John Lawrence's place, but were disappointed by the rain coming on, which continued without intermission most of the morning.

After dinner it cleared away, and we pursued our intention of going to John Lawrence's place, and called in by the way at our friend John Cox's, who was with us. Afterwards returned to Burlington, and drank tea at William Smith's, with divers Burlington friends.

3*d Day*, 26*th*.—Set off after breakfast for Crosswick's, and got to John Wright's about noon, where we dined, and so proceeded towards Stony Brook.

In the evening reached Benjamin Clark's, and were comfortably accommodated there that night—he having a good settlement, and plenty both for man and horse. 26 miles.

4*th Day*, 27*th*.—Were on the way about 7, passing by Stony Brook Meeting House. Then through Princeton, where the New Jersey College makes a spacious show, being three stories high, with about 25 windows in each. We proceeded through Kingstown, (almost gone to decay,) over Rocky Hill, refreshing ourselves and horses at Slover's Tavern. We arrived at Brunswick towards noon.

This town stands upon the bank of the Raritan, 60 miles from our city, and being so nearly central between that and New York, is fast improving.— Dined at Drake's Tavern, and then went forward 15 miles to Rahway, where we were kindly received by our friend Hugh Davids.

This day's 35 miles ride has been very pleasant, over a champaign country, under high cultivation, and the land in general productive. At one place we had a prospect of the ocean (near Amboy), which was pleasing to my son, who had never seen the sea before. Our horses performed well, and we were not much fatigued.

5th Day, 28th.—Rested well this night, as travellers mostly do, when they have good beds and are in health. Attended the Week-day Meeting at Rahway. Afterwards dined at our lodging, and took tea at John Shotwell's, after which called in to see several friends, and so went home to our quarters.

6th Day, 29th.—Spent this day agreeably with our friends. In the afternoon went over to tea at James Cox's, who is partner with H. Davids in the tanning business.

7th Day, 30th.—Being bound for New York to-day, we were stirring betimes, and on the road about 5, having a delightful morning ride to Elizabethtown, and so to the Point, as it is called, where we embarked.

After a fine run of about three hours, reached New York about 11, and were cordially received by our kind friend Benjamin Haviland and family, where we intended to quarter.

The distance across the Bay from Elizabethtown Point to New York is about 15 miles, on which we have a variety of water prospects, which were new and pleasing to my son, now about 17, in the bloom of life, and favoured with health and good natural faculties, improved (may be I may say,) by a careful education.

O may he, in his future stepping through the dangerous wilderness of this world, prefer those things which are durable, even the Divine blessing, which maketh truly rich, above all other considerations, labouring earnestly to preserve a conscience void of offence, both towards his Maker, and those whom he must necessarily have converse with in his progress through life; steadily eyeing the pointings of Truth in his own breast, so may his best interests be preserved and his end peaceful.

1st Day, *1st of Seventh month.*—Attended Meeting at New York. Our Friend Richard Titus appeared in Testimony. Dined at our lodgings.

During the afternoon Meeting a tornado arose, which was very awful and alarming, and occasioned the loss of a number of lives on the water—several small vessels being overset.

2d Day, 2*d.*—Newspaper mentions that between 20 and 30 persons were drowned near New York by the storm yesterday. We likewise understand that it extended a considerable distance southward. Our son Caleb rode out a few miles on York Island. Dined at James Parsons, and drank tea at William Shotwell's.

3d Day, 3*d*.—Walked out to see the town and markets. Fish is to be had here in great perfection. Oysters and lobsters also; but I think as to butcher's meat, Philadelphia exceeds. Dined at Thomas Dobson's, and drank tea at Thomas Pearsall's.

4th Day, 4*th*.—A rainy morning. Attended their Week-day Meeting, where Isaac Underhill appeared. Dined at John Haydock's. Received some agreeable accounts from home.

By our dear Johnny's letter we are informed that the storm last First-day was as furious at our city as here, and blew down several chimneys, &c.

Tea at Henry Haydock's. Got our horses over the ferry, intending a little excursion on Long Island to-morrow.

5th Day, 5*th*.—Crossed over the East river about 8 in the morning, having our kind friends B. Haviland and Elizabeth Haydock in company, and began our little tour on Long Island.

Passed by Jamaica, and so to Flushing, and near John Bowne's house saw the two large oak trees, under which George Fox preached to the people about the year 1672 or 3. They are nearly of one size, stand near together, and both look in a vigorous state, and I doubt not but they may continue many years to come.

About noon we reached Walter Farrington's, at Flushing, where we dined. In the afternoon went to see the entrance into the little harbour, and a large garden and nursery belonging to William Prince, which we were informed contained about 8 acres.

The Meeting House stands opposite to our lodgings, where the Yearly Meeting was formerly held;

but the House being damaged in the time of the Civil War, it is now held at Westbury.

6th Day, 6*th*.—Set off about 7 in the morning, and rode down to the sea-shore at a place called Rockaway. Had an open view of the ocean, which happened to be very calm.

We saw some bones of a whale which came ashore a year or two ago at that place, and was killed; also, the remains of two vessels which were wrecked in a storm.

Dined at Hicks' Tavern, when we proceeded towards Westbury, and crossed part of Hempsted Plains, and reached William Titus' in seasonable time in the evening, having ridden 36 miles to-day, the roads being very good and the prospects pleasant.

7th Day, 7*th*.—A fine morning. After dinner rode through Jericho to Edmund Willis' where we lodged. His house stands so high that 'tis said ships at sea may be seen when the air is clear.

1*st Day*, 8*th*.—After breakfast we left Edmund Willis' and went to Westbury Meeting, where a Friend I did not know appeared in Testimony to satisfaction.

Dined at William Titus' and afterwards went over to Thomas Seaman's, whose house was built A. D. 1688. He is a venerable old man, about fourscore, and tho' blind, or nearly so, walks to Meetings as they fall in course, without difficulty.

2*d Day*, 9*th*.—Intended for New York this morning, but were prevented from setting off by rain.— However, it cleared away about noon, and we got under way. We again rode over a part of the Plains by Hempsted Court House, so to Jamaica, where we baited. Then went on for New York, where we arrived in good time in the evening.

We had a very pleasant ride of four days on the Island, though I was a good deal afflicted with the headache.

3d Day, 10*th*.—Made a little excursion about the town. Dined at our lodgings, and drank tea at Ann King's.

4th Day, 11*th*.—Had further advices from home by our son Johnny. Dined at Thomas Mackeniss' and spent the afternoon at John Murray's. Then called in at William Shotwell's, and several other places.

After we returned to our quarters several friends kindly called to take their leave of us, we intending to set off homeward to-morrow. My son Caleb went into the salt-water bath, which is reckoned salutary at this season.

5th Day, 12*th*.—After a comfortable night, rose early, and having ordered our horses, and taken our leave of our friends, in company with two of them, we crossed the North river to the Jersey shore, and passed through a little town called Bergen.

Then over Hackensack and Passaic rivers, through Newark, the most considerable town hereaway.

About three or four miles of this road we were sadly beset with the green-headed fly, which disturbed our horses exceedingly.

Baited at Elizabethtown, and so pursued our road to Rahway (21 miles,) where we arrived about noon, and took up our quarters at our friend Joseph Shotwell's.

6th Day, 13*th*.—Dined at Hugh David's. Afterwards paid a short visit at Henry Shotwell's and Isaac Martin's.

7th Day, 14*th*.—After an early breakfast, left Rahway, Hugh Davids bearing us company a few miles. At Brunswick, 15 miles, we took a second breakfast.

Dined at Slover's Tavern, and, passing through Kingstown and Princeton, reached Robert White's at Stony Brook in the evening, and were kindly welcomed. 35 miles this day.

1st Day, 15*th*.—Attended Stony Brook Meeting. Afterwards returned to our lodging, near which the battle of Princeton, as it is called in history, during the civil war between Great Britain and America happened. Here General Mercer, Anthony Morris and many others fell. We were shown the hole where divers of them were interred.

Our kind landlord has had his wrist, two ribs, thigh and leg broken—all of his left side—and yet he remains an industrious man at the anvil, being a blacksmith.

2d Day, 16*th*.—Set out from Robert White's pretty early, and rode to Trenton, where we baited, and crossed Delaware.

We proceeded through Bristol to Thomas Stapler's, where we arrived a little after noon, a good deal fatigued. Here we were kindly received, and concluded to stay 'til next day.

3d Day, 17*th*.—A wet morning, which prevented our setting off early. However, as it broke away about noon, we took the road, and reached our habitation in good time. We have been favoured with an agreeable journey of about 27 days, without meeting with any material cross occurrence, for which we were thankful to the Great Preserver, whose providential support we had experienced in this little journey throughout.

4th Day, 18*th*.—5*th Day*, 19*th*.—6*th Day*, 20*th*.—7*th Day*, 21*st*.—Found various employment in adjusting my domestic concerns, which I do not find have suffered by my absence.

1*st Day*, 22*d*.—Was poorly part of the day, but attended two Meetings.

2*d Day*, 23*d*.—Summoned on a jury, but did go. Expect to be fined. Afternoon was much employed; I hope not unprofitably.

Wet weather and growing. Doubtless advantageous for the cultivators of the soil, whose comfort and happiness as to outward things very much depend on its produce and increase, and indeed of us also who are citizens, as our interests in some respects are intimately blended together.

3*d Day*, 24*th*.—A wet morning. Found employment about my building. Attended Monthly Meeting, which was weighty and satisfactory.

4*th Day*, 25*th*.—Poorly, with my usual complaint, but kept about with some difficulty.

5*th Day*, 26*th*.—Much engaged through the day, looking after my workmen.

6*th Day*, 27*th*.—Taken up as yesterday, and was favoured to get through some difficulties by perseverance and industry.

7th Day, 28*th*.—A busy day in various respects. Was thankful that my health was preserved through it all. Wet towards evening.

1*st Day*, 29*th*.—Attended morning and afternoon Meetings. Evening wrote a letter to one of our kind friends at New York.

2*d Day*, 30*th*.—Had a variety of concerns on hand, which kept me mostly on the move through the day.

3*d Day*, 31*st*.—Adjournment of Montly Meeting, which concluded at two sittings. Our Friend John Simpson had a marvellous time. He appears strong in the best sense, though with truth it may be said has, as it were, been raised from the stones of the street.

He has lately been twelve months on a religious errand to the Carolinas and Georgia.

Our aged Mother Elliott came to pass a few days with us; also Sister Gray.

4*th Day*, 1*st of Eighth month*.—Some encumbering affairs kept me busy, but by perseverance and industry (which sometimes accomplish great things,) I got along.

Captain Needham, from Salem, New England, arrived. Our little friend Alice did not come as expected.

5*th Day*, 2*d*.—At High Street House, our Friend John Simpson was truly eminent. His subject, love and unity. What better theme could he have spoken upon?

Brother Samuel Elliott, and his daughter Annabella, came to town from Maryland, and lodge with us.

6th Day, 3*d*.—Taken up with worldly matters. Six or eight friends dined with us. Weather fine for the season.

7th Day, 4*th*.—Much engaged in the muck of the earth. I have sometimes, yea, often, thought it was well that the law or custom of the land appropriated one day in seven to rest and religious purposes, that so mankind, as well as the lower orders of creation, might renew their strength by a necessary relaxation from labour.

1st Day, 5*th*.—Attended two Meetings. In the evening wrote a letter to a kind friend at Nantucket.

2d Day, 6*th*.—Quarterly Meeting, where I sat six hours or more, and found my weak frame much worn down. Was glad I had a house to entertain my friends.

3d Day, 7*th*.—Youth's Meeting, but found myself excused from being there, as I had been at a committee from 8 to 10.

4th Day, 8*th*.—Many engagements on hand, which fatigued me much, weather being warm.

5th Day, 9*th*.—Employed as yesterday. The sun truly powerful. This may be called hot indeed.

6th Day, 10*th*.—Heat continues by far the most intense I think this summer. I pity the poor labourers employed among the lime, &c. We hear of several sudden deaths.

7th Day, 11*th*.—The third extremely hot day this spell, so that I could do but little.

1st Day, 12*th*.—At morning Meeting, William Savery and George Dillwyn appeared. What a favour it is to be preserved in tolerable health at such a season, when the sun seems to pour his hottest rays upon the ball of our earth.

2d Day, 13*th*.—Still preserved in health and spirits, so as to proceed in conducting my outward affairs towards the desired end.

O that I may not lose sight or be slack in the most important of all concerns, as we know not the day or hour when the awful summons may be sent to our habitations.

3d Day, 14*th*.—At Week-day Meeting, which was a favoured time, G. D. and W. S. both appearing in Testimony. Went home in a shower of rain.

Dined, with my dear wife and children, at brother John's, with Brother Samuel Elliott. Afternoon to see a friend or two, who were indisposed.

4th Day, 15*th*.—Engaged about the odds and ends, gathering up the fragments. Johnny went to Stony Brook, with Ebenezer Cresson.

5th Day, 16*th*.—A beautiful, fine morning. Rose before the sun, and was ready at all points for my workmen. Nothing like taking time by the forelock, according to the common saying.

6th Day, 17*th*.—Very busy. O that I may not omit a proper attention to the most important of all business.

7th Day, 18*th*.—Warm, very warm, and relaxing to weak habits like mine.

1st Day, 19*th*.—Thrice at Meeting. Am not easy to omit them when in tolerable health, as we know not when we may be called away.

Many sudden removals happening about this time. Benjamin Penington was one of them, who I hope through infinite mercy is centered in peace, his cup of suffering for misspent time in his latter moments being very great.

O that the youth may prize their precious time, and in the morning of their days give up their names to the service of their Maker.

2d Day, 20*th*.—*3d Day*, 21*st*.—Much fatigued with worldly cares and concerns. My children probably will have but little idea of the solicitudes I have passed through for their ease and benefit, both as to things outward and inward.

4th Day, 22*d*.—Had the headache in the evening, and retired to bed early.

5th Day, 23*d*.—Had a sore night with my disorder. Did not attend Meeting, being too poorly.— Pleasant, moderate weather.

6th Day, 24*th*.—Rain in the morning; very acceptable to the languishing creation. Afternoon variously employed.

7th Day, 25*th*.—More rain in the night, which was an addition to yesterday's blessing. Was not idle this day, and felt a good deal worn down when night came. My son Johnny went in the stage-boat to Burlington Quarterly Meeting.

1st Day, 26*th*.—Weather very agreeable. Attended three Meetings, but found in the evening I had made too free with the cool air, tho' pleasant, having a hard fit of pain in my face which held me the greatest part of the night.

2d Day, 27*th*.—Towards morning the pain grew easier, so I rose with or before the great luminary, and did what I could through the day. Evening cool, which made me careful I did not expose myself unnecessarily.

3d Day, 28*th*.—Our Monthly Meeting, which concluded at one sitting, an uncommon thing of later years.

4th Day, 29*th*.—Rose early, and did a good deal of what I call business, in my private way. I find labour, in a moderate degree, truly useful to my health and mental powers.

Yet I know a care is necessary that it be not extended beyond the strength of my weak frame, for if so, experience has taught me that the effect is the reverse.

5th Day, 30*th*.—Did not attend Meeting, as I apprehended I might be excused. Tiled several chimneys in my new tenements.

6th Day, 31*st*.—Tiled two more chimneys in the morning. Afternoon, went with my dear wife to see Nicholas Waln and wife, at their country-seat near Frankford.

7th Day, 1*st of Ninth month*.—Finished tiling the new house chimneys, eight in all. The plasterers also finished their work, and we got it measured.

1st Day, 2*d*.—Sick to-day with my common complaint, so that I could not attend Meeting as usual, which was a cross. Better towards evening, though much weakened and worn with pain and retching.

Our pilgrimage through this dark vale is much checkered with afflictions of one sort or another, but if it only extends to the body, through Divine aid, it may be borne. But when the mind is defiled with sin, and the conscience wounded, the poor soul sinks, as it were, in deep waters.

O the happy situation of those who by purity and faithfulness make the Lord their friend, and feel His Holy Spirit to speak peace in hours of bodily distress.

These look through present afflictions, which are but momentary, to things which are invisible, trusting in His mercy, that at the final close of all things here below, they shall, through adorable goodness, be accepted in the beloved.

2d Day, 3d.—But poorly to-day.

3d Day, 4th.—Well enough to attend Meeting, which I hope was in some degree profitable, remarkable Ministerial labour being bestowed in good authority.

I wish to take my full share of the advice given, and endeavour to be in readiness for the all-important final summons, more especially directed to those who were advanced beyond the meridian of life, and who had not sufficiently directed their strength and talents to the most momentous of all concerns.

4th Day, 5th.—Diligence and industry enabled me to close this day to satisfaction. How invaluable is time. Let it not pass, my dear children, without improvement. What would some poor souls give for another year—yea, for a month, or even an hour?

5th Day, 6th.—Settled with and paid several of my workmen, without any jar or difference. Trouble is often prevented by making a clear bargain in the outset, and it is best to be done in writing. I recommend this precaution to my dear children in their future stepping through life.

6th Day, 7th.—*7th Day, 8th.*—Did some hard work for my feeble frame, which however, I hope, did me no harm, as I find moderate exercise, and even sometimes what may be called labour, to be better than physic, tho' I take a little of that sometimes:—one or two of Anderson's pills, or a teaspoonful or two of *Elixir proprietatis*. John Payne deceased.

1*st Day*, 9*th*.—Attended two Meetings and John Payne's funeral.

2*d Day*, 10*th*.—Much engaged.

3*d Day*, 11*th*.—Preparative Meeting.

4*th Day*, 12*th*.—Indisposed with headache most of the day.

5*th Day*, 13*th*.—Pretty well again, and found enough to do, which I esteem a favour, for there is hardly anything more tiresome than idleness, but there are few that need be so, if they are properly exertive.

6*th Day*, 14*th*.—A hard day for my strength.

7*th Day*, 15*th*.—Not much rest for body or spirit. Perhaps some who read this may think I am like a man running a race: and so I truly am, and so are you, my dear friends—a race from time to eternity—an important one indeed.

Let us, then, cast off every weight and burden which impedes us in our progress, and as we run let us pray for patience, which we cannot well do without. Patience, that most excellent virtue, which enables us to surmount many difficulties, and avoid many evils, which, without its aid, would most surely beset us in our passage.

But above all, let us get the shield of faith—a firm and humble trust in the Divine sufficiency. But this we cannot obtain without a good conscience. O may we then betake ourselves to prayer, and a watchful, circumspect attention to revealed duties, and then Merciful Goodness, who cares for even the sparrow, will enable us to step along through the various besetments attendant on human life, and in the end, if we keep our integrity, crown us with victory over all our soul's enemies.

1st Day, 16*th*.—A calm, quiet day, which afforded some refreshment. Rain in the afternoon—truly acceptable to the parched earth.

2d Day, 17*th*.—A fine, soaking rain in the night. The clouds broke away about noon. Four tenants entered my four small new buildings, which I have put up this summer.

Polly Compton died last night, after a long time of weakness. She was Hannah Cathrall's sister.

3d Day, 18*th*.—Our Monthly Meeting day, which concluded at one sitting, tho' trying to some weaklings like myself. We hear of the decease of Ezekiel Cowgill, a useful Friend of the Southern Quarter, about Little Creek.

4th Day, 19*th*.—Was favoured to feel better than common in health, for which thankfulness covered my mind. Having been so exertive through the summer, I scarcely expected it to pass without being laid up with something or other. The Lord is merciful, or we could not stand.

5th Day, 20*th*.—Finished some small matters which were not quite complete, about my new houses, and did some errands preparatory to the approaching Yearly Meeting. A number of Friends, I hear, are come from New York to this city to attend the Meeting.

6th Day, 21*st*.—Was employed in divers necessary matters.

7th Day, 22*d*.—Several Friends came to quarter at our house. Had something of my common disorder the latter part of the day and in the night.

It is a blessed thing to have an approving conscience. How sovereign an antidote against the ills of life.

If we can but get to resignation to the Divine will, and truly believe that portion of Holy Writ, that He numbers the hair of our heads, clothes the lilies, and feeds the ravens, what confidence it inspires in the Providential care of our Heavenly Father.

1st Day, 23*d*.—At three sittings at our North Meeting House, which were favoured, particularly the first.

2d Day, 24*th*.—This day our Yearly Meeting for business began, and being desired to act as Assistant Clerk to Nicholas Waln, was much taken up in that service during the course of the week, and in attention to my friends, having many at our house.

At this Meeting Rules of Discipline were made to authorize Monthly Meetings to disown such parents, guardians, &c. as consent to or connive at their children's marriages out of the order of Truth.

Also, to proceed in the same manner in cases where members deviate into the extravagant customs and fashions of the world in their dress, address, &c.

Likewise, a rule for the regulation of removals, which has long been wanting.

And further regulations respecting interments of deceased Friends, &c.

1st Day, 30*th.*—Was afflicted with the headache, but made shift to do some writing for the Meeting, which was to be dispatched early. There is always a reward for every service in the great cause of Righteousness.

2*d Day*, 1*st of Tenth month.*—Better to-day of my disorder. My son Johnny set off with Eliza Langdale, in order to visit her sister about Duck Creek—she having lately lost her husband, who was drowned.

In the evening it set in for rain, and proved a wet night.

3*d Day*, 2*d.*—Attended our Week-day Meeting. A very cool day.

4*th Day*, 3*d.*—A large white frost this morning. Busily employed most of the day, and weary when the evening came.

Life is short at the longest, compared with never-ending eternity. It is strown thick with afflictions of one sort or other, while the comforts and pleasures thereof are few in reality, and generally of very short continuance.

So that there is nothing worth setting our hearts upon but God, and nothing deserving of our unremitting pursuit but His favour, peace and acceptance in the awful hour of death, that swiftly hastens upon all flesh. "*All flesh is grass, and all the goodliness thereof is as the flower of the field.*"

5*th Day*, 4*th.*—At High Street Meeting. Not very well to-day, tho' I made out to see after some concerns of a domestic kind. Weather pleasant.

6*th Day*, 5*th.*—Poorly in health. May I improve these frequent intimations that "*here we have no con-*

tinuing city," for this poor tabernacle is evidently mouldering down to its original. To be ready, then, for the solemn close, is greatest wisdom.

Brother Samuel Elliott came to town about noon. By him we hear of the departure of Hannah, wife of Elisha Hopkins, in child-bed of her twelfth child.—An afflicting stroke to her near connections.

She was an innocent, virtuous, amiable woman, under 32, and I doubt not has exchanged a dark vale of tears for endless peace and joy.

May we who yet remain to tread the dreary path of life experience a like happy conclusion when our days are finished, is my earnest prayer.

7th Day, 6*th*.—Was troubled with a pain in my back, proceeding, I believe, from cold, so that I was mostly confined to the house.

1st Day, 7*th*.—With some difficulty I got to two Meetings, in a good deal of pain. We hear of the safe arrival at Liverpool of our friends M. Ridgway and Jane Watson, Samuel Emlen and Sarah Harrison, after a fine passage of thirty days.

Thus the devoted servants are engaged to go to and fro, that the people may be prevailed upon to attend to their most important interests.

As some have so great a portion of labour and exercise, both of body and mind to encounter, both by sea and land, it ought to be an incitement to us who are privileged to continue in our ceiled houses, to be diligent to perform the share of service allotted to us.

2d Day, 8*th*.—Continued poorly, but found employment in writing Extracts for the Meeting. 'Tis best to be doing something, being profitable for mind as well as body.

We hear of the decease of our antient Friend Thomas Carlton, of Kennet. He lived to the age of about 94. His faculties failed—so much so that he scarce knew any of his friends, and his memory was almost wholly gone.

He had been a lively Minister, of peaceable, blameless conversation, so that there is just ground to hope and believe he hath made a happy exchange.

3d Day, 9*th*.—Attended Week-day Meeting in course, tho' somewhat unwell.

4th Day, 10*th*.—*5th Day*, 11*th*.—Continued poorly, tho' not so much amiss as to be wholly confined to the house.

Had several of our New England Friends to dine, by whom we hear of the decease of our kind friend Griffith Barney, of Boston, where Thomas Scattergood and I quartered when there last summer.

6th Day, 12*th*.—A lowering morning, which produced rain after dinner. This made me think of my son Johnny, who is probably now at Duck Creek—but I hope he will not ride in the wet.

Several New York Friends set off for that place. I think they will have but an unpleasant time.

Continued poorly, with pain in my back, &c., tho' I read and wrote as usual, not being fit for much else.

7th Day, 13*th*.—Much rain in the night, and very blustering and stormy. Cleared away about noon, and was pleasant. Captain Needham arrived from Salem.

1st Day, 14*th*.—Attended two Meetings, though poorly. David Sands in town.

2d Day, 15*th*.—Rain this morning. Afternoon brother Samuel set off for home, and our son John returned from Duck Creek, having been absent about two weeks.

I have employed these several days in writing Extracts, &c.

3d Day, 16*th*.—At Week-day Meeting,—after which was held the Preparative Meeting. Afternoon engaged in writing.

4th Day, 17*th*.—Beautiful weather—mild, clear and wholesome.

5th Day, 18*th*.—At High Street Meeting, where Isaac Cox and Rebecca Shoemaker were married.— David Sands exercised his gift to the comfort of the audience.

Afternoon, attended the Meeting for Sufferings, by appointment of the Yearly Meeting, which sat about four hours on a subject of weight.

6th Day, 19*th*.—Again at Meeting for Sufferings, which sat again about four hours, and then referred the business over to next month.

Forwarded several copies of the Extracts, which I had been some time preparing, they being long this year.

7th Day, 20*th*.—Walked about a good deal, and found myself weary when night came. I desire to be grateful for the tolerable health I enjoy at present, and that so great a blessing is continued to my family.

1st Day, 21*st*.—At three Meetings. At morning and evening Meetings our Friend David Sands was eminently assisted in the exercise of his Ministry, particularly in the latter;—"*Mark the perfect man, and behold the upright; for the end of that man is peace,*" being his subject, from which he raised sound and instructive doctrine.

2*d Day*, 22*d.*—Employed writing for the Meeting.

3*d Day*, 23*d.*—At Monthly Meeting, which held late.

4*th Day*, 24*th.*—A sick day, which rendered me nearly useless.

5*th Day*, 25*th.*—Somewhat better. Made some progress in writing for the Society. Weather fine. Had some New England Friends in the evening.—Retired satisfied in having done what I could.

6*th Day*, 26*th.*—Being up before the bright source of day, I saw the most beautiful morning dawn.—Quietness and retirement has a happy tendency to sweeten the mind, and enable us to discharge the duties of life.

Laboured through the day in several engagements, and so retired, beholding all mutable things as passing clouds, which now appear, and then are no more seen—fit emblems of worldly things, which are indeed transient, fleeting and changeable, perishing with the using.

May I then lay hold on the substance, and keep an eye to those durable riches which fade not neither perish with the using.

Strengthen our faith, O Lord, in thy Divine sufficiency, and afford us thy grace, to make our passage through a world of snares and pits, unto thy Heavenly Kingdom. Went to see a sick friend.

7th Day, 27th.—Was busied writing for the Meeting. Our Friend David Sands paid an acceptable visit to our family, and spent great part of the day with us, having a comfortable sitting.

He mentioned his sense, or prospect, that though a stranger, he had to believe some present had had to travel through a large share of trouble and exercise, and many strait passes, yet under and through all the Divine Hand had supported.

Addressing himself to our sons who had been spared to us, he said he had to remember Jacob's blessing, wherewith he blessed the sons of Joseph, "*God, before whom my fathers Abraham and Isaac did walk, the God which fed me all my life long unto this day, the Angel which redeemed me from all evil, bless the lads.*"

And he had no doubt this most valuable of blessings was in store for them, if they dwelt in the holy fear of the Divine Name, and followed the counsel of Truth, as it was gradually unfolded in the secret of their own hearts.

With much more, by way of caution and encouragement to the parents and to the children. He seemed to be affectionately united to us, and to be feelingly interested in our welfare.

1st Day, 28th.—At Meeting. Called to see a sick friend or two. Had several to dine and drink tea with us.

2d Day, 29th.—Mother Elliott and Sister Gray came to spend a few days with us. Heard of the welfare of our friend and Cousin Thomas Scattergood, now on his religious visit to the Carolinas and Georgia.

3d Day, 30*th*.—At Meeting, where David Sands had some service.

We hear of the decease of Richard Shackleton, an eminent Friend, of Ireland.

Also, of great tumults and bloodshed in France, on account of the late revolution in their political government. Also, of the endeavours of several of the European powers to crush the new Constitution lately adopted by the National Assembly; as the Assembly deposed the king, and put the royal family in confinement.

4th Day, 31*st*—Was mostly within doors, part of the day being wet.

5th Day, 1*st of Eleventh month*.—At Meeting David Sands was favoured in Testimony and prayer.— Several others also appeared. Afternoon, employed in writing, &c.

6th Day, 2*d*.—Finished my writing for the Meeting, which afforded satisfaction. Every little service and labour of love has its reward, (if it be done from right motives,) in the secret of our own minds—for there is the place to receive true comfort.

The world, or those who are in its spirit, are not worth consulting. They can do us no good in the hour of exigency.

The tribunal of our own conscience must determine what is right or wrong as to ourselves, and to this I would recommend my dear children—for if our own hearts do not approve our deeds, God is greater, and will condemn them also.

Let us, therefore, "*stand in awe, and sin not.*" Otherwise, we shall be sensible of His judgments—

which will be heavier than the human mind can bear. *"The spirit of a man will sustain his infirmity"* of body; he may writhe under sickness and pain; he may combat with outward crosses, disappointments and afflictions, *"but a wounded conscience, who can bear?"*

Solomon calls it *"a wounded spirit."* He had reason, doubtless, so to speak. He had felt the indignation of the Highest for his transgressions, and spoke from the best authority—experience.

The disturbance in France, on account of the revolution in their government, and the bloodshed attending and likely to increase, is great cause of regret and sorrow to the Christian mind.

May the Almighty, if it be His Holy Will, dispose their hearts to peace and harmony.

7*th Day*, 3*d*.—Attended a Committee of the Quarterly Meeting. Called to see James Needham, who has been much indisposed some time—his brother having sailed to New England without him—which is a considerable trial.

Felt better to-day than usual, for which I desire to be thankful to the Great Dispenser of benefits.

1*st Day*, 4*th*.—Thrice at Meeting. In the evening David Sands was truly eminent on this subject: *"Keep the unity of the spirit in the bond of peace."*

2*d Day*, 5*th*.—Our Quarterly Meeting, which was conducted to satisfaction, and concluded at two sittings. David Sands dined with us, and several other Friends.

If we think we see little weaknesses and failings in any, let us be cautious of judging, but look rather to the good in all. Being sensible of our own imperfections, let us be especially careful of censuring those of others, for there is an infallible Judge that will do right.

3d Day, *6th*.—Attended a Committee at eight, and felt too much spent to be at the Youth's Meeting, to which all our young folks went.

4th Day, *7th*.—Mother Elliott and Sister Gray returned to their usual home at Brother John's, and my dear wife and self went in our chaise to Samuel Wilson's, about 8 miles, in order to attend Abington Quarterly Meeting to-morrow. We had but a cold ride—the weather indicating rain.

5th Day, *8th*.—Attended the Quarterly Meeting at Abington, where was a very large collection of Friends, and a number of the Yearly Meeting's Committee. It did not conclude 'til near five.

We just got in at Solomon Miller's, (about a mile from the Meeting House,) about dusk, where we were well entertained, and lodged in comfortable accommodations.

6th Day, *9th*.—Attended the Youth's Meeting, where H. Longstreth and Benjamin Clark had the principal service, and James Cresson prayed.

It rained heavily when the Meeting concluded, and we rode through it to Oliver Wilson's, where we dined with several other Friends. Then proceeded home, through deep and miry roads, and reached our habitation about the shutting in of the evening, and, although the weather was not pleasant, we had no cause to regret our excursion.

I reckon this to be my birth-day, on which I have completed my fiftieth year. Awful it is to consider that hitherto the Divine Hand hath been near and helped —preserving me through the slippery paths of youth.

At an early age I was left destitute of natural parents to watch over and guard my inexperienced years, when so many temptations abound, and so little judgment is formed to direct our movements.

This is the critical time, when the mind is so subject to be influenced by a wrong bias, and thereby be drawn into a labyrinth of error, from which 'tis exceeding difficult to recede or draw back.

Multitudes of objects and presentations occur to the senses, which are considered (at that age,) as desirable, but which, being brought to the standard of experience and realized, are found to be ideal and visionary, and to leave no satisfactory retrospect upon the mind; for nothing that has not the fear of God and love of our neighbour for a basis, can yield us any solid profit.

Every selfish motive and desire to gratify the sensual appetites, proves injurious to our solid peace, and when we come to be stripped of all our wretched rags of self-righteousness, nothing remains but the real treasure of a conscientiousness that our actions and conduct have been formed on the sure ground of the glory of the Divine Name and love to mankind.

7th Day, 10*th*.—Was not very well, owing, I believe, to some cold I took in my late ride. Kept house most of the day. David Sands kindly called to see us.

1st Day, 11*th*.—At Meeting thrice. In the evening our Friend Sands was drawn forth to a large audience, with great fervency and acceptance.

2d Day, 12*th*.—A fine day, but cool, and more cool towards evening. Johnny went over Schuylkill to G. Gray's, with Betsey Langdale, and returned in the evening.

3d Day, 13*th*.—At Meeting, where David Sands had a good time in Testimony and prayer. Mother Elliott came to stay a while with us.

4th Day, 14*th*.—Clear and cool. The winter now approaches our doors. Well for those who have a good stock of wood, and money in the purse.

5th Day, 15*th*.—At High Street Meeting; after which attended the Meeting for Sufferings, by appointment of the Yearly Meeting, on the subject of addressing Congress on the Indian war. The Meeting held late.

6th Day, 16*th*.—Attended at three sittings of Meeting for Sufferings, on same business as mentioned yesterday, which filled up the service of the day.

7th Day, 17*th*.—Was present at three sittings—at 8, 10 and 4—which concluded not 'til after dark, which was a good deal fatiguing to nature.

1st Day, 18*th*.—At morning Meeting, but was not well enough to go afterwards, on account of pain in my head, &c.

2d Day, 19*th*.—Attended the Committee appointed to deliver the address to Congress on the subject of the Indian war. So that business is perfected for the present.

3d Day, 20*th*.—Preparative Meeting; after which I was engaged about domestic matters.

4th Day, 21*st*.—Attended a Committee on Meeting business.

5th Day, 22*d*.—At High Street Week-day Meeting, where David Sands and others exercised their gifts in the ministry to edification.

6th Day, 23*d*.—Being wet, was detained mostly within doors, having been indisposed with a cold for some days.

7th Day, 24*th*.—Went to see our friend James Needham, who has been confined to his chamber for some days.

1st Day, 25*th*.—At Meeting, as usual. O that these frequent opportunities afforded for spiritual improvement, may not be spent in vain—for, verily, the solemn period hastens when we can no longer work, "*for there is no work, nor device, nor knowledge, nor wisdom in the grave, whither thou goest*," to which state we are individually hastening.

2d Day, 26*th*.—Was present at a Committee on the concerns of Society. Also, was employed about some affairs of a private nature.

3d Day, 27*th*.—Our Monthly Meeting, which adjourned about 2, for a week, as common. Made some progress in trimming my vines.

4th Day, 28*th*, *to the end of the month*.—Was mostly engaged within the house, the weather being cold, with sharp frosts—which occasioned me to give some further protection to my vines, by placing litter about the roots, &c.

7th Day, 1*st of Twelfth month*.—Our neighbour Smith seems near her end. (She deceased the following night).

1st Day, 2*d*.—Attended Meeting in the morning. After-part of the day wrote to a friend in New England.

2d Day, *3d*.—Thomas Barker and sister Nelly set off on their return to Rhode Island. Also, our valued Friend David Sands left the city, for his home on the North river or near it, accompanied by Brother Joshua Cresson and Samuel Emlen, Jun. Mother Elliott and Sister Gray returned to Brother John's.

3d Day, *4th*.—The adjournment of our Monthly Meeting was held, and the business concluded for this time.

4th Day, *5th*.—About this time Mary Swett, from Haddonfield, and the Friends appointed by our Monthly Meeting, viz: Samuel Smith and Hannah Cathrall, with some Elders, began their family visits to the members of our Meeting. May their labour of love receive the blessing.

I think nothing less than a sense of religious duty could induce a Friend of a small gift (though well approved,) to leave her family, and come on such an errand.

Visited a friend who has been some time indisposed. Brother and Sister Cresson visited us.

5th Day, *6th*.—Attended Meeting at High Street. Winterly weather.

6th Day, *7th*.—Was employed on some Meeting business.

7th Day, *8th*.—A very cold morning. Attended to a religious concern—endeavouring to compose a difference between two members of our Society.

1st Day, *9th*.—A clear, fine day. Johnny and his Cousin, Ebenezer Cresson, walked over to Haddonfield Meeting, with a view of staying a couple of days.

2*d Day*, 10*th*.—Employed in some Meeting business.

3*d Day*, 11*th*.—Attended our Week-day Meeting. Johnny returned from Haddonfield.

4*th Day*, 12*th*.—Engaged about my family concerns.

5*th Day*, 13*th*.—At High St. Week-day Meeting. Got in some more fire wood to add to my winter's store.

6*th Day*, 14*th*.—Took some further care to secure my vines from the force of the winter's frost.

7*th Day*, 15*th*.—A fine winter's day; and a time of general health, I believe, through the city. May we continually live under a sense of the favours bestowed.

1*st Day*, 16*th*.—Thrice at Meetings, which were comfortable to the wearied spirits, I trust, of many travellers through this thorny wilderness.

We hear of the decease of Isaac Caulke and his wife, at the head of Sassafras river, Maryland, who deceased within a day or two of each other, and were buried in one grave, about the 12th instant. An awful instance of the great uncertainty of human life. They were favoured with the good things plentifully; but nothing will bribe the messenger or prevent the stroke, when the dread commission has gone forth.

2*d Day*, 17*th*.—We hear that our friend James Needham (a Friend from Salem in New England,) has taken the small pox at John Morton's, and is likely to have the disorder very full. His case is trying, and calls for the sympathy of tender minds, which, l believe, is not wanting among a large circle of his friends here.

3d Day, 18*th*.—At Preparative Meeting. Afternoon went to see several friends, one of whom, James Needham, is sorely afflicted with the disorder mentioned in my note of yesterday.

4th Day, 19*th*.—Fine, and very fine for the season, which I endeavoured to improve according to ability. Benjamin Haviland and his son came to town from New York.

5th Day, 20*th*.—Being summoned on a jury, went to Court, but did not serve, which I was glad of.— Our friends mentioned in the foregoing dined with us.

6th Day, 21*st*.—Was employed on some Meeting business. Brother Joshua and Samuel Emlen, the younger, returned from accompanying our Friend David Sands to his own habitation.

7th Day, 22*d*.—Visited James Needham, who continues very ill indeed.

1*st Day*, 23*d*.—At Meeting twice, which I hope was comfortable and edifying.

2d Day, 24*th*.—Went to see several indisposed friends. James Needham not expected to recover.

3d Day, 25*th*.—Our Monthly Meeting, which held late. Benjamin Haviland and son dined with us.

About 3 our friend James Needham finished his earthly career, being the eleventh day from the first appearance of the small pox. He was a solid, sensible Friend and Elder, of Salem in New England.— His widow, as well as that Meeting, will no doubt be sensibly affected by his removal in the strength of his years, (about 46,) and at a time of life perhaps most fit for usefulness.

4th Day, 26th.—A number of Indians came to town, 'tis said to treat of peace. A desirable object, truly; many lives having been lost and much money expended in the contest with them. Mother Elliott much indisposed to-day.

5th Day, 27th.—Was prevented attending Meeting, which was not pleasant. 'Tis said the Indians who came to town yesterday are of the Wabash tribe, who have been among the principal actors in the war.

A man of the name of Blanchard lately arrived from France, with an intention of exhibiting a scene of folly by ascending to a great height in the air, in a balloon, which I think amounts nearly to presumption.

6th Day, 28th.—We have an account of the death of Thomas Swain, a respectable Friend near Darby.

7th Day, 29th.—The season so far has been remarkably mild, and 'tis not improbable but that we may have a moderate winter, from several concurring circumstances.

1st Day, 30th.—At Meeting thrice, to my comfort. As I have now (that is, a few weeks past,) completed my fiftieth year, the remaining span of life appears to diminish fast. I see the great necessity of preparation for another state of being which will never end. O the importance of human life, and the great events which accompany the prospect beyond the grave.

John Hopkins' wife Catharine, daughter of Joshua Howell, deceased in her prime, about 34, leaving seven children. There is reason to hope from her state of mind in her concluding moments, that her end was peaceful and happy.

2d Day, 31*st*.—Mild and moderate. River still open.

So the year 1792 ends. What another may produce none can tell. Doubtless many will be called hence and others fill their places on this changeable stage.

Happy they who are in a state of readiness for a better world in that felicity which we are authorized to believe will be the portion of all those who run the race set before them with patience, in obedience to the Divine Law placed in every heart.

NOTE.

The year 1793 was made memorable in Philadelphia by the devastations of the Yellow Fever. It carried off about 4000 of the inhabitants.

Among the many who then finished their course were Caleb Cresson's Wife and Brother. He felt it his duty to remain in the City. His son Caleb staid with him, and was attacked by the fever, but recovered.

His wife Annabella went to Radnor, with her son John, where she was attacked with the yellow fever, and died 10th mo. 12th, 1793.

His Brother Joshua Cresson remained in Philadelphia, and died of yellow fever, 10th, mo. 21st, 1793.

Daniel Offley, Huson Longstreth, Ministers of our Society, with many valuable members, fell victims to the disease. C. C. C.

Family History.

Fourth month, 1793.

I have thought it might not be improper, for the information of my dear sons, to give some little account of our family, and my passage through the wilderness of this world.

Having observed that the young generation soon lose the knowledge of their predecessors, and are scarcely capable of informing their children from what stock they sprang, or who their forefathers were.

Though I have nothing to relate that is sufficient ground for my offspring to apprehend themselves above the middle class of the community.

But I give this account from motives I think justifiable, namely, that they may not be altogether ignorant of their geneaology, and that they may see, that in the course of my life I have been cared for by the Good Hand, and though early deprived of the care of tender parents, I have been preserved by Him whose providence extends even to the sparrows, and who will provide for all those who sincerely put their trust in Him, according as He sees meet in His wisdom, which is unerring.

My grandfather, Solomon Cresson, was descended from the French and German nations—his father, as I have been informed, being of French extraction, and his mother a Low-Dutch woman.

My grandfather was one of those who were cast away on the coast of Florida, with Jonathan Dickinson and his family, in the year 1696, being then a young man about 24 or 5, and had been sent to Jamaica by his brother from New York, on mercantile business, which proving unsuccessful, and his expense considerable, on account of endeavours for the recovery of a vessel seized by the Admiralty, he was obliged to work his passage home; though he was not a sailor, as represented in the printed account of the shipwreck.

Having the Spanish language, he was of singular use to the sufferers, and perhaps one means, under Divine Providence, of preserving their lives.

He married Anna Watson, who died in 1744. He died in 1746, very suddenly, of the apoplexy, having dropped down in the street, near Friends' Meeting House in Market Street.

Being carried into his son John's in Strawberry Alley, he there soon expired. He was a turner and chair-maker by occupation, by which he acquired considerable property.

My dear father was, I think, his eldest son, and brought up to his father's calling, in which he was remarkably ingenious.

He married my mother, Sarah Emlen, daughter of George Emlen the elder, about the year 1736 or 1737.

He was industrious in his business, and generally beloved. Having gone down the river to procure rushes, he took a severe cold, which terminated in a consumption, which put a period to his life, in the 3d month, 1746, in his 37th year.

My dear mother survived him a few years, and died of the same disorder, in 1752, aged about 43 years.

They had four sons—George, Caleb, Joshua, and James. The eldest and youngest died young—myself and brother being the two middle ones. I am now in my 51st year.

Now on my mother's side:

My grandfather, George Emlen, came over, as I understand, with William Penn. He married Hannah Garrett, daughter of Samuel Garrett,* a Friend in the Ministry, well esteemed.

Samuel Garrett was also one of the first settlers, and took up his land and residence near Darby, having been a resident in Darbyshire, Old England.

George and Hannah Emlen had eight children—four sons and then four daughters, of whom my mother was the youngest, born about 1709.

My grandfather, George Emlen, deceased in the year 1710. My grandmother, his wife, in the year 1738. He was a brewer by occupation, and an industrious reputable man; and she a woman of good account for her integrity and usefulness.

---

* Elsewhere Hannah Garrett is said to have been the daughter of William Garrett, who was the father of Samuel Garrett.   C. C. C.

I was born in Philadelphia, the 29th of 8th mo. 1742, Old Style, (which, according to the present computation, answers to the 9th of 11th month).

My father dying before I was four years old, myself and brother Joshua were left under the care of our mother, who remained a widow until her decease in 1752.

She kept a shop in the house where I was born, a few doors below the Meeting House in Second Street, several years. Afterwards removed, on account of her ill state of health, with us her children, to Uncle Joshua Emlen's, at the upper end of Second Street, where she continued until her decease in the year above mentioned.

She was near two years in a declining state, and within that time took a little voyage to Rhode Island, and returned by land, having my father's sister, Mary Armitt, and her husband, John Armitt, as companions.

She also went several months into the country, amongst our relations in Chester County, but she did not receive much benefit thereby as to her health.

I was then left under the care of my Uncle Joshua Emlen aforesaid, who proved a kind friend, and managed our little estate, as executor, with great uprightness, for twelve or thirteen years, without any charge of commissions, for which acts of real friendship I hope he reaps a better reward than we could give.

After my mother's decease I went to live with my Uncle John Armitt, whose wife fulfilled the part of a kind parent to us until her decease, in an advanced age, in 1791—of whom I have written more fully elsewhere.

I continued at the school of Anthony Benezet and Alexander Seaton, until I went apprentice to Thomas Clifford, merchant, in Water Street, about the middle of the year 1757, where I served six years and upwards.

My master being an extensive trader, I had full employment, both for body and mind. I was part of the time boarded at my Aunt Armitt's.

My master had 30 pistoles as a fee, and I believe I may say without vanity, he had a good bargain of me.

In the year 1767 I formed a marriage with Sarah Hopkins, daughter of Ebenezer Hopkins, of Haddonfield, a virtuous, amiable young woman of 18, who, had she been spared to me, was likely to have made as accomplished a wife as most, but it was otherwise ordered, no doubt in unerring wisdom.

We dwelt in Haddonfield the little time she lived, about two years and four months. She deceased in the 9th month, 1769, of a fever, leaving me one child, a beloved daughter Mary.

In the spring following I returned again to my native city, and lived with my kind Aunt Mary Armitt until I again entered into a married state, 16th of 4th mo. 1772, with Annabella Elliott, daughter of John and Annabella Elliott, a family of English Friends, who came to this country from Leicester, in the year 1753. She remains my present endeared wife.

My daughter Mary deceased in the 1st month, 1777, near nine years of age. There was every prospect, had she lived, of her being all that a parent could wish.

With my present wife I have lived twenty-one years and upwards; have had seven children, two only now surviving, our eldest-born John and Caleb. The other five were taken from the evil to come in an early stage of life.

It is trying to nature to sustain the loss of children, yet it is far better to part with them in their innocency, when we have no doubt of their happiness, than to have them live and take to evil courses—for verily, the snares of life are more justly to be feared than death.

Dying Sayings

OF

Mary Armitt,

WHO DECEASED AT

PHILADELPHIA,

Second Month, 18th, 1791,

AGED 83 YEARS.

She was taken unwell the 23d of 1st month, 1791. Nothing was noted 'till the following date, when it was apprehended it might prove her last sickness.

It is believed she did not know that any thing she dropped was committed to writing.

Great care has been taken to preserve her own expressions, without addition or alteration.

1st Mo. 29th Day.

Speaking to a Friend who sat up with her, she said:—"I feel very weak, as if I was going. If I should die before morning, tell my friends I love them all. I die in full unity with them all, and love for all the world."

4th Day, 2d Mo. 2d.

Several relations present, she expressed herself thus:—"I love you all, and I hope I shall die in peace. O its a great thing to die. These poor bodies must go, and if the Lord would be pleased to speak peace to my soul—no matter how soon. I hope I shall die the death of the righteous, and that my latter end may be peace."

7th Day, 5th Mo. 2d.

To a Friend:—"I have had many low seasons the Lord only knows, I hope he will be with me in the end. The Lord preserve me in the patience."

One enquiring how she did, she replied:—"Very low. I am going to leave you, but I feel a calm—I think I may say a sweet calm. I believe I am going to peace."

To a young woman:—"It is a hard thing to die, try to be ready."

She also expressed herself in this manner:—"I am going to my Father and your Father, to my God and your God."

Afternoon, same day:—"When Christ prayed for his Disciples, he desired not that they should be taken out of the world, but that they should be preserved from the evil; and I hope I have been preserved from the evil."

1st Day, 6th.

She now kept her bed wholly, and did not set up, but as she was bolstered in the bed, she said:—"I hope I enjoy that peace the world can neither give nor take away, I do not mention it boastingly, but desire to be made thankful for it, knowing its not through any merit of mine."

After a fit of great difficulty of breathing:—"Sweet Jesus look upon me in this moment of trial."

Shortly after, to some of her nearest relations:—"I feel nothing but peace, sweet peace."

Some time after, raising her voice, she called by name a young woman who lately came among Friends by convincement, and said:—"Dear Beckey, hold fast thy profession—thee has bought the truth, don't sell it, and if thee keeps near it, it will preserve thee, and do great things for thee."

To some relations:—"The Lord be with you all, and bless you, and preserve you in love, as I have endeavoured to example you in love."

After a pause:—"The God of love and peace be with you, and keep you in love and peace when I am gone. *It's poor living without Love.*"

2d Day, 7th.

To a young person:—"Keep good company and thou wilt find great peace in it."

Same day, in great bodily affliction:—"Gracious Father be pleased to receive my spirit."

Being a little revived, she said:—"Here I am. The Lord's holy will be done."

To a relation sitting by her bed:—"O the bustle there is in the world. But, when the messenger comes we must go, and leave it all. Beware of the cumber of the world. I have been in a bustle, and thou art in a bustle. A prudent care for our families is necessary, but do not be over anxious; thee sees the time is come to me, and it will come to thee—when thee must go and leave it all."

To a neighbour:—"Thy mother was a precious woman, and we lived in great love together, above forty years, *without a jar;* and she was very careful of you. I have heard her say that she has frequently taken you up stairs, and tenderly counseled you 'till the tears flowed down your faces; and I hope thou wilt follow her good example in bringing up thy little lambs."

Same day, with great composure and awfulness, she made this

PRAYER.

"Dearest Father:—Bless and preserve all present, and let every one receive a crumb of Heavenly Bread. As formerly thou blessed the bread and handed it to thy Disciples, so let every one of us here partake of the Bread of Life, that we may all, as with the heart of one man, bless and praise thy Holy Name forever and ever.

."O dear Father, preserve the young people present, and make them to see the beauty of holiness and of purity, and the vanity of all things here below.— Place thy awful fear in their minds, that they may serve thee through life, and at the close be favoured with that peace which I now feel, and which is a great mercy.

"Praises and honour to thy Holy Name, forever and ever. Praises, praises, praises."

After a short pause, she added:—"Sweet Jesus, come. I give thee thanks for the multitude of thy mercies. Holy Father, preserve the young generation, that they may stand in awe before thee; bring them up in thy pure fear, that they may see the vanities of this world, and the beauties of true religion."

3d Day, 8th.

"Dear Johnny, love the Lord above all things."

Some time after, feeling very ill:—"May the Lord be pleased to receive me into the arms of his mercy."

After some time:—"Praise ye the Lord—praise ye the Lord; for his mercies endure forever. Praise ye the Lord."

4th Day, 9th.

"Sweet Jesus, sweet Jesus! Good is thy love, and thy countenance is comely.

Afterwards, as if contemplating on redeeming love:—"Come unto me, all ye that labour and are heavy laden, and I will give you rest."

To a female relation:—"My dear cousin, I love thee dearly. May the Lord preserve thee while thou livest, and may thou die in his favour."

To a Friend:—"Thou seest me again. I believe I am near the port."

On her taking leave:—"How comfortable the expressions of our Saviour, 'In my Father's house are many mansions.' If I could but be favoured to get within a mansion."

5th Day, 10th.

"I have often thought of those expressions of our dear Lord: 'My peace I leave with you; not as the world gives, give I.' O my dear cousin, how comfortable is that peace the Lord gives to them that love him; it is better than all the world without it. Our dear Lord said, In the world ye shall have trouble, but in me peace."

At another time:—"Sweet Jesus, have mercy on me. If it be thy blessed will, receive me into the arms of thy mercy; but thy will, not mine, be done."

6th Day, 11th.

"I can say with that great man, David, 'Though I pass through the valley of the shadow of death, I fear no evil.'"

The children of one of her near connexions being brought to her bedside, she took affectionate notice of them. Afterwards, being in the room within her sight, she said:—"I am looking at them, dear children; what a world they have to pass through. I hope (or pray) the Lord may preserve them."

1st Day, 13th.

About this time a Friend in the Ministry calling to see her, she said she loved all them that loved the Lord.

After a little pause, she brake forth after this manner:—"Praise the Lord, for his mercies endure forever. O the sweet peace that he gave to his Disciples, and is still giving unto them who follow him—not as the world gives. O Father, Father, dearest Father! sweet is thy voice, and thy countenance is comely."

The Friend then left her bedside, for she appeared to be much spent, and after taking a little refreshment, she went to take leave of her, when she put out her hand, and said:—"I love thee, and the Lord Jesus loves thee. But O the enemy is strong, but the Lord is stronger than he. Remember Job. O how the enemy desired to have him."

Then her speech seemed to falter, but soon recovering, she proceeded thus:—"O how the enemy comes in like a flood; but the Spirit of the Lord will lift up a standard against him. Great peace have all they that love the Divine Law, and nothing shall offend them."

Same day:—"Neither grace nor glory, nor any good thing, will the Lord withhold from them that love and fear him."

Soon after:—"Pain of body, but peace of mind. O Father, how good thou art; because of the savour of thy good ointment, the virgin souls do love thee."

In the evening:—"My voice is going that I can hardly speak. What a mercy that I have my senses. The Lord's mercies are exceeding great. May I praise him while I have a being."

To one who was much with her, on taking leave going to bed:—"Farewell, my dear. May the Lord bless thee, keep thee, and preserve thee every moment. He is the best Preserver."

About this time her weakness was so great that it was with great caution and tenderness she could be moved without occasioning fainting fits, in several of which her friends thought her expiring.

At times she appeared to be in great pain, yet through all manifested great composure and patient resignation. A difficulty of breathing and oppression at her breast, attended with a slight fever, and sometimes hard fits of coughing, was what she laboured under, so that she frequently requested the chamber door to be opened.

Nature gradually weakened, and the lamp of life but glimmered in the socket, now and then emitting a clearer light, and again sinking almost to extinction.

2d Day, 14th.

"Father, be pleased to take me into the arms of thy mercy. I return thee thanks for the multitude of thy favours. My tongue is too short to praise thee. May all present join in the triumphant song—the triumphant song."

To one who had the special care of her :—" Dear Betsey, the Lord will bless thee. Don't look to man for help, but look to the Lord, and he will bless thee forever.

4th Day, 16th.

About this time, or it may be a little earlier, she spake sensibly and pertinently to one of her family whose welfare she had at heart, giving her good advice and caution, and left several sweet and comfortable messages to absent friends, whom she never expected to see again in mutability.

She ordered several legacies to be added to those in her will, and having a concern on her mind for the good of some who she was not likely to see, she desired two in particular might be sent for, and when they came, she was enabled to discharge herself in much love and Christian meekness.

5th Day, 17th.

About 6 P. M. she was raised in her bed with great difficulty, and being extremely weak, she audibly expressed:—"'The righteous hold on their way, and men of clean hands grow stronger and stronger.'— May you all grow strong in the Lord, and in the power of his might."

Many savory sentences which she dropped are omitted, as they were not penned at the time they were spoken. Indeed, it may be said in truth, that her heart seemed continually indicting good matter, and when her speech almost failed, she had at times utterance given to admiration, and (all vain boasting apart,) her peaceful closing moments preached to the bystanders, affording proof that she had not run in vain, nor laboured in vain.

The fear and terror of death were removed, and she met the awful messenger with that calmness and peaceful resignation that is often vouchsafed in adorable mercy to some of the Lord's chosen and faithful servants.

On the dawn of day, having a glimpse of the stars through the curtains, after a laborious night, she said:—"The morning stars sang together, and all the sons of God shouted for joy."

6th Day, 18th.

Being the day of her departure. As the day broke she seemed as one waiting for the coming of her Lord, her lamp trimmed and light burning.

On receiving something to take, she expressed feelingly:—"Praise ye the Lord, for his mercies endure forever."

A relation from the country coming in and drawing to her bed, about two hours before she died, she expressed great love for his wife and children, and said again:—"Praise ye the Lord, for my tongue is too short to praise him."

A little after, in broken accents, the powers of speech failing, moving her hand towards him, (I. L.) she uttered with difficulty:—"He hath brought me to his banqueting house, and his banner over me is love," and on taking leave, desired he would give abundance of love to his dear wife and friends that way.

This was an affecting scene to the friends and all around her bed.

Within about an hour of her departure, she said: "May the God of love and peace be with you all."

A little while after, she said:—"*It's all peace—it's all joy forevermore.*"

These were her last words, except desiring to be turned, or motioning for a drop of water, or something of that kind.

Within a few minutes of her death, her speech being gone, she motioned with her fingers for those near her to come and take their leave. On their kissing her, she endeavoured to move her lips to several in return, manifesting the strength of her love to the last.

About half after eleven, in the forenoon, she finished her earthly course, without groan or struggle— having been eminently favoured in every stage of her illness, and also in the hour of death, by that Gracious Hand that was her support and preservation through life, and her defence and crown in the solemn, awful conclusion.

Thus our endeared friend finished her earthly pilgrimage in full age, as a shock of corn cometh in its season. Having maintained the warfare, she was mercifully crowned with the victory over all her soul's enemies.

It remains to add a word or two for the information of those who were least acquainted with her, and for the encouragement of humble travellers in succeeding days, who may be conflicting with the perils of time, and continued to finish the momentous work of their souls' salvation, that so they may be fitted for an abundant entrance into their Heavenly Master's Rest.

She was the daughter of George and Hannah Emlen, born at Philadelphia, the 1st of the 11th mo. 1707–8. Her father died in 1710, and she was carefully educated by her pious mother, being the seventh of eight children her father left.

In 1728 she became the wife of our valued Friend John Armitt, who deceased in 1762. Thenceforward she remained in a single state.

In early life she was distinguished for circumspection of conduct, sweetness of disposition, gentleness of manners, and comeliness of person.

Being favoured to choose that better part which our blessed Lord spake of, she in future time was rendered a bright ornament to our Christian profession, conspicuous for love, charity, meekness. These, with other spiritual graces, adorned her life, and gained her general favour, both within and without the pale of our religious community.

For the Truth, as its sanctifying operations in devotedness of heart are submitted to and obeyed, never fails to make its humble followers honorable in private life, and more openly in the view of all who value Heavenly Wisdom for its innate perfections and the benefits resulting to its happy possessors.

She was favoured with an even, peaceful progress through a length of years; favoured of her great Master; happy in herself, because free from conscious guilt. She passed the youth, meridian and decline of life, but little ruffled with the adverse storms which are so generally attendant upon worldly things.

Having no offspring of her own, she was exempt from some of the cares and solicitudes which possess a parent's breast; nevertheless she was as a parent unto many, and failed not in the several duties incumbent on those who are entrusted with a charge so great as nurturing souls for Heaven, and the Divine blessing was not withheld from her pious endeavours for the lasting benefit of those whose education fell within her sphere.

Experience made her wise in the best sense. The Law of the Lord was in her heart, and its happy influence was manifest; few of her steps did slide. She loved the Lord, and feared before his Name—therefore his promises were fulfilled to her. She was fed inwardly and outwardly. His covenant was with her, of life and peace. He gave them to her for the fear wherewith she feared him, and was afraid before his Name.

I am not disposed to over-rate her endowments. Yet 'tis Apostolic advice, "Render honour unto whom honour is due." It's true, she needs it not; she has slept in Jesus, therefore has the Lord brought her unto glory! Nevertheless, many remain to tread the thorny paths through time. Let her example animate —let her virtues encourage all—the youth especially.

The prize, the inestimable prize, is worth contending for—at every expense, at all hazards—and (through holy help, blessed be the Lord,) is attainable. It will cost us something, yea, all worldly things, yet the purchase even so were cheap. For, if haply we are enabled to lay hold on eternal life, we shall possess what is above all price. But failing therein, earth with all its perishing joys, and delusive, momentary delights and pleasures, will leave us wretched —yea, most miserable indeed.

I now return to the deceased.

Her light shone in life and in death—brightest at the solemn close. She disclaimed all merit, yet was made rich through free grace, for thereby alone she was enabled to withstand, and having done all, to stand! She acknowledged her unprofitableness, but was accepted in the beloved. Her works praise her in the gate, and being dead, she yet speaketh,—and what is the language of her life and death? Go thou and do likewise. Sell all, and thou shalt inherit eternal life.

She died 6th day, 18th of the 2d month, 1791. Her remains were accompanied to High Street Meeting House, 2d day, the 21st, (having been an Elder above forty years,) where the Master's presence was vouchsafed to a crowded audience: Heavenly Bread was dispensed to the multitude. Her example was held up to surviving pilgrims, and the voice of the Spirit was:—"Weep not for me, but for yourselves and for your children."

She was then respectfully attended to the grave, and committed to the dust.

But her sanctified spirit has, we trust, ascended unto Him who gave it—even to join that *great multitude which no man could number*, which that favoured servant, John the Divine, saw before the Throne, of *all nations, and kindreds, and tongues, and people*, with this triumphant song:

"AMEN! BLESSING, AND GLORY, AND WISDOM, AND THANKSGIVING, AND HONOUR, AND POWER, AND MIGHT, BE UNTO OUR GOD, FOREVER AND EVER. AMEN."

www.ingramcontent.com/pod-product-compliance
Lightning Source LLC
Chambersburg PA
CBHW021841230426
43669CB00008B/1043